UNSEEN DEPTHS
OF THE HEART

Tales of an African Dynasty

Book One

BABATUNDE OLANIRAN

First Printed in United Kingdom 2021

Published by Conscious Dreams Publishing
www.consciousdreamspublishing.com

Cover design by Alexis Chivir-ter Tsegba and Jerry Wolf
Edited by Karolyn Herrera and Elise Abram
Book Interior and E-book design by Amit Dey

ISBN: 978-1-913674-49-6

TÍ EYE Ò BÁ PA EYE MÍRÀN LÁRA,
OJÚ ÒRUN TÓ EYE FÒ LÁÌ FARA KANRA.

* * *

If one bird won't bother another,
the sky is wide enough for them all to fly.

Contents

ONE

———◦•◦———

On a very warm morning in the little town of Ìkirè, located in the lower Guinea Region of Africa (southern region of modern-day Nigeria), the beautiful rhythms of the birds—especially those of the *òdèré kókó* (palm doves)—gave the quiet surroundings a feeling of living existence. The subtle wind blowing through the mango and cocoa trees produced divine sounds as though the leaves and the wind were conversing. Red-headed agama lizards and bush rats were excited at the sun's gradual rising, as shown by the speed at which they ran in and out of the entrance holes they'd drilled into their mud homes. As the sky grew brighter, a new day began. Husbands and wives awoke. Mothers woke their children, and all forms of life rose up for the new day.

Most men of Ìkirè villages in this era were either farmers, hunters, or healers. Their wives usually stayed at home to do chores, cook, and take care of the children. Cries of some of the younger children resonated from one house to the other as their mothers screamed out their names to wake them up. As the day's activities unfolded, older male children prepared to farm with their fathers, and the older females picked up their calabashes and headed for the stream to get the family's water for the day.

Ìkirè was a part of a larger community in the lower Guinea Region, which had once been part of the Òyó Empire, the historical birthplace of the Yorùbá people. The village was bordered by other villages, such as Ìbàdàn, Apòmù, Orílé-òwu, and Gbòngán. In the last part of the nineteenth century, the British colonial masters had already begun visiting the region, strictly for business and exploration purposes. Formal education and proper forms of trading had not yet been established.

Farmers with smaller farmlands cultivated their crops, mainly to feed their families, and those with larger farmlands traded their produce with other farmers in neighbouring villages. Trading was carried out mostly through the exchange of goods of value, popularly known as trade by barter. The only two types of informal education available in the villages were provided by farmers, teaching their children how to farm through the seasons, and healers, called *babaláwos* (father of the mysteries), who used tree bark, leaves and incantations to make herbs for treating the sick and curing diseases. The healers, in particular, were the teachers of this time, and they were very much revered in the village. It was not uncommon for fathers to send their children to learn from these healers.

In Ìkirè, as in every other village, the *Oba* (King) ruled the village and had a staff and council of elders. Kings managed all the affairs of their villages and oversaw and owned everything on their land. The King made and enforced the laws through his army which protected the King's palace, village, and people. Aside from the King, who was more often than not the most revered and respected man in the village, men with large farmlands, prominent healers, and men of honour also commanded respect and were consulted in affairs of the communities. Young men grew up ambitious, wanting to expand their fathers' lands, acquire knowledge, marry the most beautiful women in the villages and expand their families.

For these reasons, disputes often surfaced. Land disputes were rampant. Families clashed with each other. Sometimes, this led to individual—and sometimes mass—killings and death. Over time, it was solidly established that the strong always had a better chance of surviving and prevailing over the weak. A man had to be strong and wise to be a champion in these communities.

King Adéorí of Ìkirè was not the wealthiest amongst his peers who ruled other villages although he was highly respected and adored by kings from near and far. Known widely for his sharp intellect, spiritual gift, and powers, he was one of the only kings of the time whose cabinet of elders contained the most powerful priests, spiritualists, and healers in the region. His late father and grandfather were famously known as great spiritualists of their times, and Adéorí followed judiciously in their footsteps. As a young man, before succeeding and ascending to his father's throne, he was loved by everyone in the village of Ìkirè because of his passion for people and their well-being. To some of the villagers and outsiders, this would explain why he mostly surrounded himself with spiritualists and healers ready to take care of his people whenever they had any ailments, sicknesses, or predicaments.

He always said, 'My kingdom and people do not own the biggest farms or have the most wealth, but I know that as long as we are alive and healthy, we will gain wealth and improve our land. If not in my own time, we will get there in my children's time.'

King Adéorí's palace sat on about six acres of land in the village. As modernization gained prevalence in the area, some of the wealthier kings in neighbouring Ifè and Òyó had demolished their palaces—which had been built with mud—and rebuilt them with polished wood and concrete to emulate modern buildings. These structures were stronger, looked better, and were more expensive to erect. The kings spent enormous amounts of wealth, generated from highly successful taxpayers in their villages, to make their dreams of reconstruction and the renovation of their palaces come true. At a time when mud houses were common, only two kings had houses built of concrete, and it was a symbol of great affluence and opulence. King Adéorí often discussed building a new palace with his council of elders, but as he was the king of a smaller village with few successful farmers—few enough to be counted on the thumb of one palm—he could not afford this luxury just yet.

One thing was certain: he was focused and strong-willed. He had over five hundred slaves who worked tire-lessly under his direct command every day. Rumours of the British colonial masters' possibilities of expanding their trade in the region and seeking more farm produce for export had spread. So, like the big rulers, King Adéorí had his ear to the ground, and he knew he must be at the forefront of the party as soon as trading began. The King knew the colonial masters would come sooner or later and that the work and effort put in by him, his sub-ordinates, and the slaves would not be in vain, and they would create massive benefits for the whole village in the years to come.

The King was fifty-six-years-old and married to two women: Adéòsun and Adénìké. He'd married Adéòsun, his first wife, immediately after ascending to his father's throne twenty-six years ago, at the age of thirty. Adéòsun was nineteen years of age when she'd married him. Unlike King Adéorí's father and many other kings and men of the time, Adéorí had vowed to marry only one wife and keep his family simple.

When his council had proposed that he marry a sec-ond wife, and not for the first time, he always said, 'I am a man of one wife, and I want to marry only one wife so I can live longer than my father who passed away at the age of fifty-four.' Some council members raised arguments that marrying multiple wives had not been the reason for his late father's untimely death, but Adéorí responded by saying, 'I have lived in this palace day and night with my father, the King. When no elders or anyone else sat around him, I did. When he spoke out loud to himself in the wee hours of the morning and the late of the night thinking nobody could hear him, I did. I think I am in the best position to know what might have been the cause of my father's untimely death.'

Unfortunately, the topic of the King's marrying a second wife persisted when Adéòsun did not bear any children with Adéorí, and the pressure and tension from the council of elders increased, year after year. The King knew and understood the importance of having a successor, and there were so many things he would like to teach his son or daughter, just as his father had to him. Adéorí and Adéòsun tried to have a child for years to no avail. At the age of fifty, after twenty years of marriage to Adéòsun and no cry of a baby in the palace, Adéorí finally heeded the advice of the council to take a second wife. He spoke to Adéòsun about his decision to take a second wife.

Knowing how important it was for him and the lineage to have an heir to the throne, she gave him her full support. She cried for weeks, but she was happy to give him her full blessings to go ahead.

King Adéorí married his second wife, Adéníké, at the yearly farm harvest festival celebration. Adéníké, who was twenty-five and arguably the most beautiful lady in the entire village, moved into the palace. The only child from a modest Ìkìrè family, she'd lost her father at the age of thirteen and was thereafter raised by her mother. She was a typical example of *omo tí wón kó dada tí ó tún ara rè kó* (a child that was properly raised who heeded advice and also thought well of herself), and she was very respectful and worked hard to support her mother. Before she married King Adéorí, she had not known any man intimately, and she quickly won the King's full affection because of her beauty and sheer innocence. Unfortunately, after six years of marriage, she was also unable to give King Adéorí an heir.

The inability of the King and his wives to bear a child had become more than just a problem for the palace, and every citizen of Ìkìrè was concerned. The council elders were concerned. Other rulers—who were allies of Ìkìrè Kingdom—were also concerned. The predicament slowly turned to embarrassment. The King was not getting younger, and he understood the implications of not having an heir to succeed him. The likelihood that the throne and kingdom ascending to and being ruled by Adéorí's ancestors would come to an end after centuries increased. Without an heir to succeed him, he would be forever remembered by history as the king who could not procreate to keep his family's dynasty alive.

After the yearly harvest celebration in 1899, King Adéorí summoned a meeting with the council of elders, which was unusual and much like requesting a state of emergency. Ideally, the council members took a fortnight break after the celebrations before the start of the new farming season, but in this rare occasion, the King had called for a meeting the following day, and the council members knew the reason for this must be extremely important. The King also summoned the three great priests in his kingdom and five of the greatest seers from neighbouring villages to attend.

TWO

————◈◈◈————

A ll council members and priests arrived promptly at the meeting the next morning. As usual, the meeting was held at the most important venue in the King's palace. The council meeting room was considered by some to be the most sacred and important place in the kingdom. It was where the monthly council meetings were held to discuss all issues pertaining to the kingdom and beyond. Adéorí's seat in the council room stood high above those of the council members. The great sculpture of Adélànwá, the first king and founder of Ìkirè, Adéorí's great ancestor, graced the centre of the council room. Council members paid tribute to the great King Adélànwá by bowing and saying a quiet prayer before taking their seats at the council table.

Members sat around the King's throne in a circular fashion. Smaller sculptures of past kings also graced the sides and corners of the room. It was widely believed that the spirit of King Adélànwá and all other past kings were present at all council meetings to guide decisions made by members. This belief was further buttressed by the fact that the corpse of the first king was buried beneath his likeness at the centre of the council room. One important task for every new king ascending to the throne was to ensure the face of his predecessor was moulded on his sculpture, presented, and placed in the council room amongst kings from the past. This task was typically the first thing a new king would do once he was sworn into his position.

All fourteen council members were seated with the eight priests and seers who had been asked to join. The welcome trumpet blew softly for about a minute, and King Adéorí stepped into the council room. All twenty-two members present stood and bowed their heads to acknowledge the King's arrival. Adéorí walked to his throne and commenced the meeting, almost immediately.

'Thank you all for making yourselves available for this meeting on such short notice,' King Adéorí began. 'May the spirit of our great ancestors who are present with us on this day and every other day guide us through today and the days to come.'

The council members replied almost as one voice, '*Àse Oba* (Amen, Your Majesty).'

'You may all be seated,' said the King. The members settled into their seats, and the King continued.

'My honourable council members, I am sure you might be able to tell that there is a vital reason for why I have summoned you all today. An issue has proven unsolvable over the years, and I strongly believe that the time to find a lasting solution to this problem is now. *Ìyá mi* (my mother), the great queen, always told me that no matter how tough or difficult a problem might seem to solve, we will never need to visit the heavens to find a solution for it. All solutions to all problems are here on earth.'

The members nodded their heads in agreement.

'I have also asked the messenger to inform you all to come prepared today because we will remain here together to find a solution. We will call upon our ancestors and gods. We will call whatever or whomever we know how to call, and most importantly, we will put our heads together until we overcome this huge obstacle facing us.

'As you all know, it's been over twenty-six years since I was crowned the king of our great land, and I have also been married for this long to my first wife. Because of our inability to have an heir, and after years of persuasion from most of you, I married my second wife, Adéníké, about six years ago. A marriage that I imagined would bear fruit and bring joy to the palace and kingdom at large has turned out to bring more pain, greater doubt in our capabilities, and the need for urgent attention and a solution.

'All of my ancestors were succeeded by their own flesh and blood, and this must continue during my era and those of my future generations. I was born as the fruit of my father's loins, and it is only right that I bear my own fruit into this world before my demise.'

The council members nodded their heads again.

King Adéorí continued, 'My question for all of you distinguished members of my great council starts with what we should do. How do we go about solving this situation? How do we ensure that my time in this kingdom does not fall on the bad side of history? I know we have tried physical and human solutions that have obviously failed. A spiritual solution is the next way forward, and we must seek out and ask our gods so that we might receive. Drastic times require drastic actions, and if we cannot find solutions to our own problems, who will?

'As you all can see, we are joined by seers from our kingdom and neighbouring kingdoms to help ensure that no stone remains unturned in our quest to find a resolution to the situation.'

When King Adéorí had finished, a grave silence filled the room, the type of silence that felt like inaudible conversations were going on in the room. The council members and priests were mostly elderly men who had served on the council during the time of Adéorí's father, and they were all very knowledgeable. Adéorí's words had struck them so hard that they had almost immediately begun to deliberate, seeking out a spiritual solution to the predicament. The main qualities of their king of which they all knew were his relentlessness, his drive, and that he would go to any and every length to make sure he found a solution.

After about five minutes of continuous silence, Ìkirè Kingdom's high priest stood to speak. He began with greetings and praise for the King: 'Tribute to the gods, our ancestors, and spirits of the great kings of our kingdom,' he said. 'I pay my tribute to Your Majesty, our great king, the reason why the fearless becomes fearful. I also greet you, all fellow council members. May the wishes and blessings of our ancestors rain on us all and on the great Kingdom of Ìkirè.'

'*Àse* (amen),' agreed the council members.

'You have spoken well, my King,' the high priest continued. 'Our people say that when a shoe is tight and hurts the foot, it is the person wearing the shoe that knows precisely where the shoe hurts the foot. The truth is that this pain hurts all of our feet and the feet of those in our great kingdom. The consequences of not solving this issue would be grave, and they would affect each and every one of us. We have dirt in our eyes, and we must all work together to remove this dirt before it makes us go blind.'

Nodding and murmuring commenced among the council members.

'With your permission, Your Majesty, I would like for us to debate this issue among ourselves and with the gods of our land for *wákàtì meta* (three hours). We can then continue the meeting with some of our proposed findings and solutions after the allotted time, Your Majesty. I assure you that the heavens will open its doors to us, and we will find a solution,' said the high priest.

'Thank you, *agbenu òrìsà nla* (mouthpiece of the gods),' the King replied. 'Thank you for your undivided service to our great land. You have spoken well. Do any members have anything to add or anything contrary to say about the high priest's suggestion?'

The council members shook their heads to indicate that they had no objections to the high priest's suggestion.

'In that case, I hereby postpone the meeting to be continued after three hours.' The King rose from his seat and the council members stood with a bow as the King found his way out of the council room.

The council members immediately began debating the situation.

Shortly after the King had left the council, three palace guards and two hostesses walked into the council room with jars of wine, kolanuts, and fruit to entertain the council members. Council members sat in groups and whispered to each other as they discussed the issue at hand. The priests sat close to one another as they began consulting the gods with prayers and incantations and the casting of cowries on white sand.

The process of problem-solving for the council was divided into four phases. As practiced during periods of predicaments and despair, the priests—led by the high priest of the kingdom—began the process of problem-solving by consulting the spirits and gods of the land to find out the reason and cause of the problem. Once the reason and cause had been established, the second phase began. The priests resumed consulting with the gods and spirits of the land to seek possible options and solutions to the diagnosed problem. After the options had been discovered, the third phase began, with the priests discussing these options with the King and other council members.

Council members continue with the third phase by trying to unanimously decide on one option or a combination of options as a solution to the problem. If a unanimous solution was reached by the council members, the King—who had the final say—would validate and accept the solution, and the priests would commence the fourth and final phase. In a situation where the council members were not able to reach a unanimous decision, a vote would be proposed that had to be approved or disapproved by the King. Just as with a unanimous decision, the King needed to validate the vote of the majority before a solution was finally accepted. At the fourth and last phase, the high priest sought direction from the gods of the land and the spirits of the ancestors for the appropriate strategy to be utilized and direction on how to implement the agreed upon solution.

THREE

---•◦•---

Meanwhile, daily activities went on as usual in the palace.

It was now almost nine o'clock, and the sun was out. The presence of guards around the council meeting room indicated that a meeting was ongoing; aside from that, the morning was the same as every other morning as palace staff engaged in chores and moved from one corner of the building to the other. The palace was divided into three sections: the residence section, the administrative section, and the staff and security section. The residence section was where the King and his queens resided. King Adéorí had spent six months redesigning the residency to contain three different chambers before marrying his second wife, Adénìké. The King's was the largest of the three, and he wanted to ensure both queens had their own spaces in the palace so as to avoid conflict between them. The residency chambers were elegantly built and decorated, inside and out.

Queen Adéòsun, the King's first wife, stood in front of her chambers. She still looked strong and beautiful, even as she'd aged over the years. The Queen had been in charge of the palace's domestic activities since she'd married the King all those years ago. She was highly revered due to her kindness and commitment to the kingdom, especially when it came to empowering and helping women, children, and the less privileged. Everyone knew how much the King loved her because of the way he showed his true affection for her, both in private and in public. This had earned her the nickname *amóba rérìn*, which meant 'one who makes the King smile,' by the palace staff and amongst women and men across the kingdom. Just as on most mornings, that morning was not an exception, and she stood elegantly, about to perform her usual routine, giving orders to the heads of the palace's domestic staff.

Speaking in a soft but commanding tone, Queen Adéòsun instructed: 'My husband, the King, is having a meeting today with the council members. While chores are ongoing in the palace, I want you all to make sure that they are done quietly and with caution, especially chores around the council meeting room and in the administration section of the palace.'

The heads of the palace's domestic staff nodded in unison to show their understanding.

The Queen continued. Speaking to the head of the kitchen staff, Queen Adéòsun said, 'Olúbùnmi, please make sure you have every kitchen staff member on standby. The council meeting will likely last longer, so please ensure there is enough for the council members to eat and drink. Lunch and dinner should also be taken into consideration so that if the meeting lasts well into the day, all of that may be duly taken care of.'

'Yes, My Queen,' Olúbùnmi responded. 'I have already asked the staff to prepare a few things to entertain the council members for a start, and we will continue to make preparations.'

'That's good. You may all resume your duties now,' the Queen concluded.

The heads of the palace's domestic staff responded together as they bowed their heads and said, 'Thank you, My Queen.'

The heads of staff made their way from Queen Adéòsun's chambers, meeting Queen Adéníké, the King's second wife, on their way. They greeted Adéníké, but just as she had done most mornings, she ignored the greetings and kept walking towards Queen Adéòsun's chambers.

The friendship between the queens had grown distant over the last year, largely due to the younger queen's insolence toward the older queen. They had confronted each other several times to exchange abusive words of discontentment. This discord was fast becoming a pronounced rivalry between them, day after day, and was evident not only to the King, but also to the members of the palace. Adéníké had become more demanding of the King's time, and she wanted more of his attention.

Her wish was to have the King and the palace to herself, and she despised the power and control the King had bestowed upon Queen Adéòsun over the palace's activities, including those concerning some of the women's affairs in the kingdom. As much as Adénìké knew that the older queen had managed these duties since before the King had married her, she had continuously complained to him over the past year about how she'd felt neglected by him, and that more attention and powers had been given to the older queen in the kingdom.

The first major rift between the queens had happened two years after the King had married Adénìké. Queen Adénìké had asked the King to allow her to create a foundation to support young women since she was fast becoming a role model to them in the kingdom. The King, who liked the idea very much, had asked her to collaborate with Queen Adéòsun who had already established a foundation spanning across the kingdom and beyond, so that Adénìké could leverage all of Queen Adéòsun's years of work and experience and both queens could work together. Indeed, a vast number of young women were already within reach of Adéòsun's foundation. Aside from leveraging what the older queen had put in place, the King had emphasized the need for togetherness when it came to activities coming from the palace, and he wanted to avoid anything that might create differences between his queens. He had told them that working jointly was perfect, as it would solidify their bond and bring them closer together.

Both queens had initially agreed and had been excited to work together to create a larger force. Adénìké had shared her plans with Adéòsun, and they had commenced almost immediately, for the good of the kingdom. Unfortunately, barely six months in, Adénìké began complaining bitterly to the King about how Adéòsun had refused to acknowledge some of her most important plans. She went ahead to complain about how Adéòsun only wanted things done her own way and had treated her as a subordinate, rather than work together in a partnership as the King had asked them to do. The King had intervened a few times, but after a year, when the situation had seemed to worsen between the two women, Adénìké had decided to quit working with Adéòsun. Both queens had valid claims, but unfortunately, this had been the inception of hundreds of tiffs and quarrels ensuing between them over the coming years.

Despite their differences, Adénìké continued to give Adéòsun her due respect as an older woman and the first queen of the kingdom.

Adénìké walked elegantly past the staff who had just taken orders from Queen Adéòsun. At thirty-one, she was vibrant, radiant, and extremely beautiful, considered by all as a woman with a perfect figure, and she always walked with her head held high above her shoulders. She had a modern perspective on life and was growing and developing into a wise queen herself. Her fair and beautiful skin colour was captivating, and she had the power to attract any living thing. She stole the show wherever she went yet never attempted to be the focus of all eyes' attention. Everyone was attracted to her, men and women alike, especially the younger women and girls who followed her and wanted to be like her.

Queen Adéòsun was still standing in front of her chambers, looking at some plants when Adénìké approached. 'Good morning, Olorì Àgbà (Older Queen),' greeted Adénìké. 'I hope you had a good night.'

'Good morning, dear Adénìké,' Queen Adéòsun replied. 'Yes, it was good. Adúpé (thank you). How was yours?'

'Adúpé, mo sùn dada (I slept very well).'

'Glory be given to the gods of our land. What brings you to me this morning, my dear?' Adéòsun enquired. 'I hope everything is okay.'

'Yes, everything is fine,' said Adénìké. 'I will be travelling to Ede to visit my friends this afternoon. Months ago, we planned to have a reunion for seven days, starting today, but I totally forgot. I received a message from my friends that they had arrived in Ede very late last night. I went to the King's chambers to inform him this morning, but he was not there, so I came to ask if you have seen our husband this morning, Olorì Àgbà?'

Adéòsun answered, 'Yes, I saw the King earlier this morning. He summoned a meeting with the council of elders, and they started very early. I think you must have gone to check on him while he was with the council members, but now, he should be in the palace garden, performing his morning devotion.'

'I wasn't aware there would be a council meeting today,' Adénìké said with a sober frown. '*Oko wa* (our husband) usually notifies us two or three days before council meetings are held. I wonder why he did not tell me anything about it. I hope I haven't done anything to upset him.'

'No, Olorì. I only heard about the meeting this morning as well.' The King had sent Àlàbí, one of his personal guards, to inform the Queen and all domestic staff about the impromptu meeting. 'Àlàbí said the meeting was very important, and the King wants everyone, including you and me, to stay in the palace until the meeting ends. Àlàbí was to inform you immediately after he left me, but clearly, you have not received the message yet.'

'It sounds like a very important meeting. I did not receive the message from Àlàbí, but at least I am getting it from you now, Olorì. As the King wants us to be around until the meeting ends, I hope it ends soon enough so I can leave in time to travel to Ede.' Adénìké paused for a moment. 'I will go see if our husband is in the garden now so I can tell him of my trip. Thank you, Olorì Àgbà, I will inform you before I depart. I wish you a good morning,' she concluded as she left Queen Adéòsun's presence.

'I wish you the same, Olorì,' Queen Adéòsun replied.

King Adéorí had just finished his hour-long morning devotion, a common traditional practise performed by rulers of the great kingdom and one that had existed for centuries. It was a special time of the day when the King reflected and connected with the gods of the land and his ancestors, and it was frequently referred to as 'the King's daily moment of divinity'. Kings were known to perform their devotions in the palace garden due to its natural feel and serenity. As long as the King was present in the palace and not travelling, the morning devotion was a vital part of the King's daily routine. King Adéorí's late father had always emphasized the importance of the devotion, from Adéorí's teenage years onward. The King never failed to remember that his father had commonly spoken of the morning devotion as the primary moment of balance in every king's day.

Adéorí had settled in his chambers and was sitting majestically on his throne in the room in which he received visitors and guests. Jagun, his chief of defence, had brought updated news about ongoing land disputes among some of the kingdom's farmers and those in the neighbouring Kingdom of Òsógbo. Farmers in Òsógbo Kingdom had forcefully and unlawfully reclaimed lands that had been legally purchased by Ìkirè farmers a few years back. The Ìkirè farmers had called on the King who, because of his love and passion for his people, had to interfere to restore peace and seek proper justice.

King Adéorí had been informed of Jagun's arrival by one of the palace's guards, so he had decided to see him to get the most recent updates about the dispute situation before returning to the council room to see how far along the council members were with the other issue he'd raised.

Jagun walked into the King's presence with six of his men. He prostrated himself to greet the King, and his men followed suit. While still prostrate, Jagun and his men declared, '*Kábíyèsí o* (one who does not yield or surrender to anyone).'

Adéorí gestured with his staff to ask the men to stand and take their seats, and the men settled into the seats in front of the King. Just before Jagun had begun to give the King his report, in walked Queen Adénìké, and all seven men stood up to greet the Queen. King Adéorí waved his staff towards Jagun and his men, indicating they should step out into the waiting area while he talked to the Queen, and the men bowed their heads and followed Jagun from the room.

Queen Adénìké walked towards the throne and closer to her husband. She knelt in front of him to greet him while he placed his palms on her shoulders. 'Good morning, my husband and My King, the King of our great Kingdom, the King of Kings and King of Queens.'

King Adeori responded with a smile. 'Good morning, my beautiful Queen, *Aya Oba* (wife of the King), and my pride. How was your night, and how are you today?'

Queen Adénìké replied, 'My night was fine, my husband, and the morning is going well.'

King Adéorí pulled Adénìké up gently as she rose from her kneeling position to sit beside him. 'I sent Àlàbí this morning to inform you about an impromptu meeting I had called with the council of elders,' the King explained. 'As you know, due to the traditions of our land and those of my forefathers, every member of the palace, including myself, is expected to be present within the premises of the palace until the council meeting has concluded or adjourned. I cannot know yet how long the meeting will last, but I will rejoin the council members once I finish with Jagun.'

'*Olówó orí mi* (the one who paid and owns my dowry),' Adénìké began, 'I must have missed Àlàbí this morning, but I just left Olorì Àgbà's chambers before coming here, and she told me about the meeting in progress. I went to Olorì Àgbà to find out your whereabouts because I'd gone to your chambers earlier this morning to inform you about a trip I would like to make to Ede to visit with my friends. Two months ago, my friends and I had planned to meet today in Ede, and I forgot about it entirely until late last night when I received a message from my friends, who arrived in Ede yesterday, so I came to seek your permission to go visit them, my husband. I plan to be away with them and return in seven days.'

The King said, 'All right, My Queen, but you will need to wait until we finish or adjourn the ongoing council meeting. As soon as you are able to leave, I will assign four guards to go with you to Ede in addition to your entourage. Hopefully, the council meeting will not last too long and disappoint you. On the other hand, you may also ask your friends to come here to the palace to spend time with you. We could arrange for guards to usher them here, and of course, they would be met with the best hospitality.'

The dismay Adénìké felt was apparent by the expression on her face. Whenever something disheartened her, it was obvious to others, and especially to the King. She knew that planned council meetings sometimes took as long as twenty-four to forty-eight hours. An impromptu meeting indicated that the issue raised was important, and the meeting could last even longer.

Having discerned her distress, King Adéorí told her, 'I can see that you are unhappy, Olorì. These meetings are very important for us and our land. It is also crucial that we do things the way they are done so we can reach the desired outcomes. The duration of the meeting is out of my control, but in the meantime, why not consider asking your friends to spend time with you at the palace? I am sure they will understand.'

Queen Adénìké insisted, 'My King, my friends have been to the palace a few times to visit me, and it is my wish to leave the palace to visit them this time. This would be a good break from all that is going on in the palace as well as from the recently concluded celebrations. I should have left yesterday to visit the full seven days—if I do not leave today, the trip will not have been worth the journey because I will have already lost one day. My King, I will wait until the late afternoon, but if the council meeting has not finished by then, you will need to make an exception for me to leave.'

Knowing how adamant Olorì Adénìké could be, especially when she had her mind made up to do something, the King shook his head and responded, 'I know how you feel, My Queen, but you must remain in the palace until the council meeting has concluded or adjourned. This is how we have done it for generations, and it will not change today. I will not insist on holding you back if you decide you must go while the meeting is still ongoing, but remember that obedience of what is right is better than making sacrifices to correct wrongdoings.'

Adénìké stood up and left her husband's presence, unhappy. In her thoughts, she was determined to do as she wished when she walked out of the large visiting room.

King Adéorí watched her as she angrily left the room. He whispered to himself, 'My beautiful, adamant wife who is always ready to neglect tradition to do what she pleases. Oh, well, I cannot force her. May my mother's spirit guide her to make the right choice today.'

The King summoned Jagun and his men back into the room, and their meeting continued for approximately an hour more.

FOUR

————•••————

At fifteen minutes past midday, the council members were still debating in the council room. The palace kitchen staff, headed by Olúbùnmi, had just served the members palm wine, kola nuts, and dodo-Ìkirè, a small but delicious appetizer made from plantains originating in Ìkirè Kingdom. Through the leadership of the high priest, all priests had successfully completed the first phase of determining the cause of the predicament. The eight of them had separately consulted the Ifá Oracle, and to their surprise, they had received the same results as to the cause of the predicament that had befallen the kingdom. Only on rare occasions have all priests came up with the same findings in the Ifá's initial consultation. Usually, when the Oracle is consulted by multiple priests, the Ifá determined multiple reasons for the cause of the problem. These reasons were sometimes revealed to different priests at different times of consultation. All findings from the Oracle would then be considered, discussed, and a solution—or solutions—would be sorted. In this case, all eight priests had seen the same outcome from their Ifá.

The situation made the predicament both simple and complex to solve. Simple because it had become very clear from where the problem had stemmed, which helped provide focus towards where and how to seek the solution. It was also complex because when the same outcome was revealed by Ifá to different priests as the cause of the same problem, it was a huge sign of the intensity and magnitude of the problem. The complexity signaled that a ready solution was possibly unavailable, and in the case where a ready solution *was* available, it would typically be difficult to obtain and with stringent repercussions and dire circumstances.

The council members waited for the King's return to the council meeting room with worried looks on their faces as they consumed their wine and dòdò Ìkirè. As the members worried, the high priest reminded them that King Adéorí, the great ruler of Ìkirè Kingdom, was a king of very strong will, and where there was a will, there was always a way.

King Adéorí walked into the council room to resume the meeting, accompanied by five personal guards. All council members rose to their feet and bowed their heads as the King went to his seat at the centre of the council room. Adéorí sat on his council throne and asked the members to take a seat.

The council members settled back into their seats, and a minute of silence was observed in the room.

King Adéorí spoke first: 'Thank you all for your time and dedication. I hope the palace's staff has provided enough entertainment and are making sure your needs are met. The wine is of great quality, and hopefully, not kicking in yet,' the King smiled.

Chief Adébulé responded, 'Yes, Your Highness. The wine tastes excellent. We're not tanked up yet, but we are getting there, little by little.'

The other members of the council laughed. Some cheered, holding up their cups of wine. The King was known to make light of difficult situations to ease the stress and tension in the council room.

'I am glad the wine tastes good,' continued Adéorí. 'So, my esteemed council members, do we have any progress yet as to the predicament at hand?'

The high priest stood to address the King's question. He cleared his throat and began: 'Thank you, My Lord. May the gods of our past kings and ancestors never let us encounter problems that are larger than life and too large for us to solve.'

'Àse,' responded the council members.

'Yes, Your Majesty. We have been consulting the gods of our land, our ancestors, and most especially, Ifá. We have also been discussing the situation together since you last left us. The other priests and I have each consulted Ifá in our own ways and shared the outcomes of our consultations with one another and the other council members.'

After clearing his throat, the high priest continued: 'Your Majesty, coincidentally, the outcomes we have all seen through Ifá are the same, which indicates a very strong sign, My Lord. What we have learned is that the second king of our great Ìkirè Kingdom—your great-great-grand-ancestor, King Adélékè—was faced with the very same problem of not being able to birth an heir to take over his thrown. Ifá, the great Oracle, has also told us that King Adélékè faced this inability to have a child for forty years, but after the kingdom priests of the time consulted with Ifá and the gods of the land, they were able to find a solution, and King Adélékè welcomed an heir into the palace to inherit the kingdom.

'Ifá told the priests at that time to perform specific spiritual rites and rituals in order for King Adélékè to produce an heir. These rituals were to be performed in parts. Part one was to be done before the Queen conceived. Part two was to be done seven months into the Queen's pregnancy, and the third part—the most important—was to be done when the child turned-seven-years-old.' The high priest paused briefly for the King to take in the information.

King Adéorí paid close attention when the high priest continued: 'Your Majesty, our findings from Ifá suggest and confirm to us that the third phase of the ritual, which should have been performed when the child turned seven-years-old, was not performed by King Adélékè. Although we do not know why this ritual was, unfortunately, not performed or the circumstances surrounding what happened at that time, Ifá has told us that, without a doubt, the consequence of not performing the rites and rituals when King Adélékè's heir turned seven years of age is the inability of present-day Ìkirè Kingdom's throne to bear an heir.

'These are our findings, Your Majesty. May the blessings of our forefathers and ancestors continue to guide Ìkirè Kingdom and direct us onto the right path forevermore.'

'Àse,' agreed the council members.

A silence fell over the council room. The King took a deep breath, contemplating all he had heard. He could not understand why his direct ancestors would have made such a grievous mistake, but who was he to judge? Without them, he would not be there in the first place. He remembered the adage he'd recently shared with Queen Adénìké: *Ìgboràn sàn ju ebo rúrú lo,* which meant no type of ritual performed to solve a problem is better than being obedient and avoiding the problem in the first place.

'Thank you very much, high priest of Ìkirè Kingdom. I also want to thank all members of my esteemed council for your patience and dedication to our great kingdom and to my reign. *Ní agbára olódùmarè, èsè baaba kò ní gbérí kó tún wá se lórí omo o* (by the power of The Almighty, the sins of the father shall not surface and then manifest on the sons).'

'Àse Oba,' said the council members.

'My esteemed council, now that we know where the shoe hurts our feet, how do we go about finding a solution to extinguish this plague on my family and the unborn generations to come?' implored the King.

Olúmo was the deputy high priest, who was ordained to serve in the absence of the high priest and was also in charge of leading the second stage of the problem-solving entailing consulting the Ifá Oracle to seek possible options and solutions to the problem that had been diagnosed. He'd also served as a prominent member of King Adéorí's father's council and was highly respected by all men in the region. Olúmo stood to speak: 'I greet you, My Lord and Majesty, the Great Lion and Ruler of Ìkirè. Thank you for giving us the opportunity to serve you and our kingdom the best way we can. I also greet you, my fellow council members. Our forefathers always say, *Eni tóbá bèrè ònà kò ní shi ònàgbà* (the person who asks for directions will not go in the wrong direction). We will consult Ifá and ask the Great Oracle to guide and direct us to the right solution to solve this problem, once and for all. My colleagues and I will get back to work, and as soon as we have good news, we will relate it all to you, My King.' He looked around the room at the other council members and asked, 'Have I spoken well, members?'

The council members nodded. Some responded, saying, 'Yes, you have, Olúmo ńlá.'

'Thank you, Olúmo ńlá and my great council, the great pillars of our kingdom. We will resume the meeting again shortly.' The King rose to leave the council room. As usual, all members of the council rose and bowed their heads as he walked from the council room followed by his guards, accompanied by the sound of a flute.

The council members immediately reassembled to start the second stage of consultation with Ifá.

At 3:30 p.m., activities in the palace had begun to slow. The sun still shone brightly in the sky, but soon it would begin to set, and the evening would gradually arrive. The day after the yearly farm harvest festival was usually calm and restful due to the intensity and energy that had been put into both the preparations and the festive event. The calmness of the surroundings was felt in the palace and was reflected in the kingdom as a whole. The only serious event occurring was the council meeting at the palace about which only members and palace workers knew.

More often than not, the slaves spent time together in the evenings after the day's work to play sports, such as wrestling and football, or table games. They lived together as one big family, which was contrary to the existing custom dictating that slaves should be treated unjustly and maliciously. King Adéorí's leadership was based upon the premise that everyone was a human being first before anything else, and he had enacted laws ensuring everyone, including slaves, better treatment and entitlements in his kingdom. Due to the low intensity of work during the two-week break that had just begun, palace slaves engaged in different fun and entertaining activities organized at the palace to keep busy.

One palace tradition that had survived the centuries was the *pankration* competition organized by the King's guards, a unique mixture of full-contact wrestling and boxing. This competition was the most popular and anticipated contest during the break, and sixteen of the kingdom's strongest slaves participated. On the final day of the tournament, the King, queens, council members, and citizens of the kingdom came together to grace the occasion, and a winner emerged. The winner was awarded a prize, and the King bestowed upon him the title of *Alágbára Lárìn erú* (the most powerful amongst slaves). The winner also served as the head of all slaves for the year and would hold the title until the next pankration tournament.

Some of the slaves had gathered in the open field behind the staff and security section of the palace to practise and prepare for the preliminary rounds, which would last four days, after which sixteen men would be selected to participate in the main contest. Oláolú, the current champion and two-time winner, was also practising on the field. He had won the pankration tournament for the last two years, back-to-back, and was widely seen as the favourite to win this year's contest, as well. Oláolú was handsome and attractive, to say the least. He had a slim build, and while not very muscular, he possessed extraordinary fighting skills. He was also very intelligent and could perform the most difficult tasks with ease. Oláolú had become popular and well-known among the slaves the year before he'd won his first pankration title when he'd finished as the third runner-up and immediately caught the attention of the palace and other citizens in the kingdom, but especially, Queen Adénìké. Oláolú had become the Queen's favourite slave, and she never failed to send for him whenever she needed things done, both within and outside the palace.

Two palace guards arrived on the field where the slaves had gathered to watch the practise and demanded Oláolú's urgent attention. Oláolú, who was currently in the middle of a match with his close friend, Àdìó, stopped and walked through the crowd of onlookers towards the two guards.

Oláolú, who was sweating profusely, said to the guards, 'Good afternoon. May I ask why I have been called upon this afternoon?'

'Good afternoon, Oláolú,' one of the King's guards replied. 'We are here to inform you that Queen Adénìké demands your immediate presence in her chambers. The Queen demands that you get ready and bring along three other slaves because you all will be travelling with her to Ede. The Queen plans to set out in thirty minutes, and she expects your presence before then.'

'Very well. I will gather the others, and we will go to her chambers immediately,' Oláolú replied, upset at the impromptu call. He had silently wished that nothing would disturb his practise for the competition, but there was nothing he could do at that point. Although, as the previous winner, he had automatically qualified for the main contest and did not need to participate in the preliminaries, he liked to take part in them, regardless, to warm up for the main competition. Hopefully, this trip would only last a day or two, he thought, as he walked towards his room in the staff building.

He called Túnjí, Gbadé, and Àlàní to his room, briefed them on the Queen's request, and asked them to get ready at once. The three men he had chosen had no interest in participating in the wrestling competition, and they were also his friends. They were the right ones to bring with him at that time, and they were expected to meet him in the common room within the next fifteen minutes.

FIVE

———◆———

Queen Adénìké walked into her husband's chambers, and the guards at the entrance bowed their heads in respect. She approached the visiting area, and the staff on duty told her that after lunch, the King had gone to his room for an afternoon rest as he usually did about ten minutes before.

Queen Adénìké proceeded to her husband's room and knocked gently on the door before going in. She walked through the beautiful, well-lit room with the finest decor available, and towards the King's study to find Adéorí sitting in his chair, going over some old manuscripts. The King raised his head to see his beautiful queen walking towards him, and he smiled a boyish smile. It was not exactly clear to the Queen whether his smile meant that he knew why Adénìké was there or if he was surprised to see her.

She walked over to him and went down on her knees to greet him. 'My King, my love, and the King of All Kings— good afternoon, and how is your day going, My Lord?'

King Adéorí's smile grew broader, and he responded, 'Very well, My Queen. Your words bring me joy. *Báwo ni aya Oba* (How are you, My Queen)?'

'I am doing well, my darling husband,' Adénìké said.

'Great! I am glad,' said the King. 'I sense that you are here to tell me you still intend to embark on your trip to Ede to visit and spend time with your friends. If that is truly the case, my wishes remain the same.'

'But, My Lord, this visit is very important to me, and I want to go. I promised my friends I would be with them. I will also travel with guards and slaves for proper help and protection.'

'There will be no dispute, Adénìké.'

Adénìké knew the King rarely called her by her name unless the situation was serious.

King Adéorí continued: 'You know I would never impose anything on you or force you to do anything against your will. I believe you should have a mind of your own and listen to your voice of reasoning. This has nothing to do with protection—this is about tradition.

'Yes, I called an impromptu council meeting, but no one may leave the palace until the meeting is closed or adjourned. I will not stop you if you intend to abide by your own wishes, but understand that *Èmi ò lówó ní nuè* (I do not support it).'

With a tone of finality in his voice, the King recited the proverb, '*Ajá tó ma sonù kò ní gbó fèrè olóde* (the dog that goes missing will never hear the whistle of the hunter).'

Adénìké pleaded, 'I have to go, My King. Please, allow me!' before rising and leaving the King's study room.

Adéorí watched her as she walked out. As always, he knew she would do whatever she'd made up her mind to do. Sometimes this served for good purposes, but other times, it served the wrong ones. He knew that this time she was wrong, but he prayed silently to himself and hoped that she would be guided on her journey and not incur the wrath of the gods.

Adénìké hurried back to her chambers. Oláolú and three other slaves were waiting for her outside. She went in to finish her preparations for the trip. Two chamber maids—who would also be accompanying her on the trip—were completing the last bit of packing. Adénìké, a highly demanding queen, would normally require luggage enough for anyone else's full week's trip when she only planned to travel for two days, so the amount of packing needed for the seven-day trip to Ede was unimaginable.

The two guards who had gone out to the field to summon Oláolú arrived at the Queen's chambers with her chariot, pulled by two horses. The guards would ride the horses pulling her chariot, leading the envoy on the journey while the four slaves would follow behind with two additional horses.

Ten minutes later, the chamber maids carried the luggage outside, and the slaves loaded them onto the chariot. Queen Adénìké departed from her chambers in a beautiful, royal dress with matching head ties and beads, the guards helped her step into the chariot, and they all rode out of the palace to begin the hours-long journey.

The council members requested the King's attention in the council room at eight o'clock that evening after a rigorous exercise of continuous consultation of the Ifá Oracle and divinities of the land had been conducted in search of a solution to the problem at hand. King Adéorí arrived at the council room twenty minutes later to discuss the findings with the council members. Although it had been a long day of discussion and consultation for the council members, they had grown accustomed to doing this over the years, and they all viewed it as a duty to their fatherland, strongly believing that the ends always justified the means.

On occasions when meetings lasted for days, council members retired for the evening at eleven and began again at seven the following morning unless they were required to stay longer or overnight. In the given situation, this might appear to be the case. It was definitely not the toughest problem they had tried to solve—in some cases, figuring out the cause of the problem had taken four to five days—so from all indications, this particular situation seemed to be moving on accordingly.

King Adéorí walked into the council room along with his guards. The council members rose and bowed their heads as the King approached his throne and sat. The

King gestured to indicate the council members could take their seats. One of the guards whispered to the King, and then he and the rest of the guards left the council room, leaving the King and his council members alone.

Deputy High Priest Olúmo, who had taken charge of the second phase of problem-solving, got up to address the King and council members. 'I greet Your Majesty,' Olúmo began, 'the brave and utmost ruler of our great kingdom. Thank you for honouring our call almost immediately. We all know that you continuously attend to other matters pertaining to the kingdom as well as the one we are working on here. May Olórun—the owner of the heavens—and the gods of our land proffer to you the strength and wisdom to lead this kingdom to the promised land.'

'Àse,' affirmed the council members.

'Thank you, Olúmo and esteemed members of my council,' said the King. 'Thank you all for your dedication to my legacy and our great kingdom.'

'All thanks goes to you, our Dear King,' Olúmo responded. 'We are always happy to be at your service and the service of our kingdom. Over the past few hours, the council has consulted Ifá continuously under watchful eyes.' The deputy high priest gestured to include the high priest and himself. 'Ifá has directed us to a part of the solution to the problem at hand, and the solution will involve a sacrifice to Ifá and the gods of our land. We called for your presence to begin deliberating on the solution and some of our findings so we can find a common ground and commence the sacrificial process.'

'*Nkan tó bá ti yá kì tún pé mó* (once it is time to do something, there is no reason for any more delays). I am all ears, Olúmo. What are the proposed solutions received from Ifá?' King Adéorí asked.

'*Esé* (thank you), Kábíyèsí. Ifá's demands in this situation were very straightforward. The final ritual that King Adélékè and his queen failed to perform when their son—your great-grand-ancestor, Adétànwá—turned seven-years-old must be fulfilled. Ifá made us understand that a special *ose dúdú* (black soap) and *kònkòn* (traditional sponge) were prepared with a mix of concoctions from the earth and given to King Adélékè's wife. For the first part of the ritual, the Queen was required to bathe with the black soap for seven days without setting her eyes on anyone. On the eighth day, she was required to see the King first thing before the sun rose, at which time he made love to her. By the grace of the Olódùmarè, the Queen conceived a few weeks later.

'After the first ritual, the Queen was required to keep what remained of the black soap and traditional sponge in a safe place, where no living being would ever set their eyes upon it because it would be needed for all three stages of the ritual. The second part of the ritual, to be performed when the Queen was seven months pregnant, required her to wash her pregnant stomach for seven days without setting eyes on anyone, and she was to do it with the traditional sponge and black soap she'd used before she'd conceived. Just as with the first stage of the ritual, the Queen was to keep the traditional sponge and black soap in a safe place so it could be used for the third and final stage of the ritual.' Olúmo paused for a moment before continuing.

'Ifá has also shown us that the Queen performed the second ritual successfully, and Adétàńwá was born. The third ritual was to be performed when baby Adétàńwá turned seven-years-old. The Queen was expected to pay homage and thank Òsun, the goddess of the river and fertility, by visiting the tip of the Òsun River with her son, Adétàńwá, on his seventh birthday and washing his head seven times with the water from the flowing river, using the same traditional sponge and black soap. She should have used up the remaining black soap for this stage of the ritual, then thrown the traditional sponge into the flowing river, said a prayer with her son, and thanked Òsun, the river goddess. Unfortunately, for some reason unknown to us, she passed away at the age of thirty-three, which was about six months *before* her son's seventh birthday, and the last stage of the ritual was never performed. Obviously, her husband, King Adélékè, never attempted to arrange a remedy for failing to perform the last stage of the ritual.'

The King and the council members remained attentive as Olúmo narrated their findings. When he was done, King Adéorí shook his head in amazement and surprise. He knew that when these rituals were not conducted or concluded properly, severe repercussions were usually the result.

'So, how do we fulfil this final ritual so the curse can be removed from my lineage and our kingdom?' demanded the King.

Olúmo hastily replied, 'There is a solution, Your Majesty, although I must say that the gods are very angry. Some warning signs have been shown to past kings during their reigns to amend this deed, but none have been able to do so. Either they did not see these signs clearly, or they saw the signs but did not heed their warnings. As our fathers say, '*Eni tóbá wo bàtà lómo ibi tí bàtà tiń ta lésè* (it is the person who wears the shoes that knows where they hurt the feet).' I am happy because the patience and wisdom of our Great King will see us through as we find a lasting solution to this. Ifá has only given us one way out. It is a difficult way, but we should be able to abide by it if we follow Ifá's directions accordingly.

'We must prepare another ose dúdú and kònkòn from the same combination of concoctions used for the late Queen, Adétàńwá's mother. We must also find a male descendant from King Adélékè and Adétàńwá's bloodline. He must be taken to the Òsun River and have his head washed seven times as a tribute to the river goddess. After this, we must thank Òsun, say a prayer, and also ask for the goddess's forgiveness for delaying the final stage of the ritual. In addition, only a reigning queen of our great kingdom who is no older than thirty-three years of age— the age at which Adétàńwá's mother passed away—can perform the final rites of washing the head of the male descendant from the King's bloodline to appease Òsun, the river goddess. Ifá has also made it known to us that for this ritual to be accepted and for the King to have an heir, we must perform this amendment ritual before the rising of the next sun.

'The final piece of information received from Ifá was that tragic news would be received in the palace seven weeks after the ritual has been performed, and the King must accept the news without becoming upset or showing any form of anger. After this incident, one of the queens shall conceive for the King, and we shall hear the cry of a child in the palace once again. These are our findings, My Lord.' Olúmo breathed a relieved sigh while looking around the council room at the other members. He bowed his head towards the King and settled back into his seat.

The council room was silent as King Adéorí processed all he had just heard, and he stood up and paced around the room, murmuring to himself. After several minutes, he walked back to his throne and sat down. 'The gods of our great kingdom will always be with us,' uttered the King. 'They have spoken, and Ifá has spoken. We have very little time to make all necessary arrangements for the execution of the ritual rites. I am the only surviving male from the bloodline of my forefathers and the only one fit to represent the child whose head must be washed. I assume that we need to consult Ifá to see whether a sitting king can fill this role. Ifá has also said that only a queen who is no more than thirty-three years of age can perform the rites. Only one of my two queens—obviously, Adénìké—may fill *that* role.

'Olúmo, the sacred one,' King Adéorí called out. 'Will you consult with Ifá immediately to see if it would be acceptable for me to perform the head-washing rites?'

Olúmo, the high priest, and the other six priests proceeded to the centre of the council room to sit on their goatskin mats. They sat together in a circular manner, facing each other to begin saying prayers to Olódù-marè and the gods of the land as they commenced their consultation.

King Adéorí signaled to the two men guarding the entrance to the council room. One of them approached immediately, and the King quietly spoke a few words to him. The guard withdrew, then returned quickly with the head of the King's guards, and King Adéorí gave some instructions to him, and he left the council room.

The King sat on his throne as the priests continued with their consultation. He appeared fairly relaxed as he watched the priests carry out their duties, yet the look on his face made it obvious that he had a lot on his mind. He secretly wished that Queen Adéníké had not yet embarked on her journey because if she had, it would prove a major obstacle to fulfilling the rites before the next sunrise. Knowing Adéníké as well as he did, he was certain she would have already left for her trip, but he hoped otherwise. Adéorí also wondered why Ifá had said the ritual must be performed before the next sunrise, but then he reminded himself that the ways of the gods were different from the ways of man, and most times, inexplicable.

Council members talked in low tones with one another while the Ifá consultation continued. Òtún, the King's right-hand man, and Balógun, the chief warrior and generalissimo of the King's army, went to King Adéorí to discuss a few things with him.

After about fifteen minutes, Olúmo got up from his mat and called for the attention of the King and council members. Before Olúmo could begin speaking, the head of the King's guards returned to the council room to deliver a message to the King. The guard was brief and left as soon as he was done.

'*Oba wa olúbùsólá àti gbogbo àwon ìgbìmò ìlú mo kí yìn o* (Our King, the one ordained by God to wealth, and all the council member chiefs: I greet you all),' Olúmo said. 'We have good news. Oba Adéorí can perform the amendment ritual rite, and the gods, by the grace of olódùmarè (The Almighty), will accept our sacrifice.'

'Àse, Olúmo,' said the council members.

'We will begin arranging for the procurement of the items needed to prepare the black soap and traditional sponge immediately. We must also inform Olorì Adénìké so that we can begin preparing her for the task at hand before the sunrise.'

King Adéorí interrupted. 'Olúmo and council members, we have a problem. Olorì Adénìké has embarked on a trip to Ede. The head guard has just confirmed it. She knew she was expected to remain at the palace until the council meeting concluded.'

'Èwò (abomination)!' Olúmo and some of the other council members exclaimed. The council members looked stunned.

Òtún stood up to speak. 'Your Majesty, we need to act fast. Ede is an eight-hour journey away. How can we reach the Queen in time? Even if we send out guards immediately to inform her to return, it is certain they will not return here before sunrise. What should we do?'

The council members met the news of Queen Adénìké's absence from the palace with dismay. None of them needed to consult a soothsayer to understand how long it would take to travel to Ede and back. Even if the King himself decided to go to bring back the Queen, it would make absolutely no difference. The most important piece of the ritual was missing, and something needed to be done about it.

After a short silence in the council room, King Adéorí cleared his throat to respond. 'Òtún oba (the right hand of the King), there isn't much we can do about bringing the Queen back to the palace before sunrise. It is now almost 10 p.m., and it has been barely four hours since her departure. It would take at least fourteen hours at the earliest for the guards to reach her and return with her, and this would obviously be pointless.'

King Adéorí then called on the high priest and deputy high priest. 'Agbenu Òrìsà ńlá, Olúmo, can we find out from Ifá whether there is something we can do about the Queen's absence from performing the ritual?'

The priests began another session of consulting the Ifá oracle as proposed by the King. All eyes were on the high priest and his deputy as the consultation progressed. Fingers were crossed, and some of the council members said quiet prayers to Olódùmarè with the hope that Olódùmarè would bestow his infinite mercies and another way out would be found.

King Adéorí also observed as the priests chanted incantations to Ifá to ask for guidance and direction. After about ten minutes, Agbenu Òrìsà ńlá and Olúmo communicated with one another, and not long after that, the high priest lifted his head to speak to the King and the council: 'Your Majesty, the King of our great kingdom. May you live long, My Lord. I also continue to greet you, my fellow council members. Ifá has once again made known to us that the only way out of this predicament is for a queen of the land, who is not older than thirty-three, to perform this ritual before sunrise. If this is not done, the King risks the chance of not having an heir, which we all know will lead to grave circumstances. In light of this situation, the only solution available—and we must act on it very quickly—is for the King to marry a new wife who will be presented as a queen of Ìkirè Land tonight. The new queen will then perform the ritual before sunrise, and I am sure that, by the grace of Olódùmarè and the gods of our land, our sacrifice will be accepted.'

SIX

The room went silent again. King Adéorí gazed at the ground, lost in thought. If only Adénìké had listened to him!

After a long moment of graveyard silence, King Adéorí returned from his thoughts, lifted his head, and spoke. 'This is highly unfortunate, but what needs to be done must be done. This is an unusual way for me or any king of our land to choose a queen, but drastic times require drastic measures. Any woman who would agree to be a queen of our great kingdom to solve our problem at this trying time will forever be remembered not only as a queen, but also as a blessing and a solution for us and generations to come. We will need to coronate her as queen tonight, under the rights and laws of our land, and sometime in the coming weeks, we will conduct a proper ceremony as has been done for any new queen of our kingdom. I believe the next question,' stated the King, 'is how do we find a new queen tonight?'

Chief Oláòsebìkan, the Basòrun who was the head of the council chiefs and next in rank to the King, stood to speak. The Basòrun had been quiet for most of the evening as he usually only spoke to settle disputes or proffer solutions. He was known as a brilliant man, and usually the first one King Adéorí consulted about the most serious and daunting of issues. He was considered the King's best friend by most people, both inside and outside the kingdom. Chief Oláòsebìkan and King Adéorí had been very close friends since childhood and were groomed in similar ways. He had taken on the position of Basòrun after his late father—who had also served as Basòrun to King Adéorí's father—had passed away barely three weeks after the King's father had passed.

'Long live Your Majesty, ruler of our great Ìkirè Kingdom,' said Chief Oláòsebìkan. 'I bow to you, My Lord.' He bowed to the King and continued. 'I bow to Olódùmarè, the creator of the heaven and the earth. I bow to the gods of our land and our ancestors. Your Majesty, thank you for giving each of us the opportunity to serve on your council and be a part of the solution to this predicament. I strongly believe and pray to Olódùmarè that we will see this through together, and we shall all live to rejoice in the end with the cry of an heir in the palace.'

'Àse,' agreed the council members.

'My Lord, I want to use this opportunity to offer my daughter, Olúfúnké, to you in marriage to be your queen and help fulfil the sacrificial rites to remove this uncomfortable mucus trying to block our collective nostrils. I do this for the love of the throne and our kingdom, and if Your Lord permits me, I will go immediately home to discuss this with my wife, my daughter, and the rest of my household because this must be decided with them face-to-face to seek their full consent. As we know, *ojú lòró wà* (when the eyes meet is when real conversation happens). The clock keeps ticking, and we only have a few hours to prepare so many things, but only with your permission shall I proceed to discuss this with my family.'

Everyone knew the Basòrun would do anything to make King Adéorí happy and ensure his reign's success. Their friendship was like that of the tongue, and the teeth—whatever touched the tongue would most likely touch the teeth, and whatever affected the King would likewise affect the Basòrun.

'Basòrun, *olórí àwon ìgbìmò ìlú* (head of the council of chiefs), *okùnrin méta* (three men in one),' responded the King. 'The step you have chosen to take on behalf of this kingdom and the kingdom of our forefathers is great. We do not have the luxury of time to debate many of these issues, but your sacrifice today will be remembered for generations to come, and it will be rewarded immensely. I do not need to say much at this moment, but with the consent of the council members, you may take your leave to discuss this sudden development with your family.'

The council members agreed at once. 'Yes, Your Majesty.'

'The Basòrun has all of our support and full consent,' said the high priest.

The Basòrun—Chief Oláòsebìkan—left the council room to go to his family.

'Agbenu Òrìsà ńlá, Olúmo, and all esteemed council members—let's begin preparations for the initiation of the new queen and gather all the items needed for the rites and rituals. I thank you all for standing by me and our kingdom in these dire circumstances.

'I must leave to speak with Queen Adéòsun while the preparations commence.'

'Kábíyèsí o,' the council members answered.

The King called over the head guard and whispered directions before rising from his throne, stepping out of the council room, and proceeding to his chambers.

Queen Adénìké and her envoy had been travelling for almost five hours without stopping. She had remained awake throughout the trip, enjoying the beautiful scenery and vast landscape, one of her favourite things to do. She wasn't able to travel often enough to enjoy the beautiful work and scenery created by Olódùmarè in the western region. Thoughts of the King had frequently crossed her mind, and they were her only distractions from enjoying the view. She felt as if two voices were speaking to her about the conversation she'd had with her husband. One voice spoke to her from time to time at the back of her mind, telling her that she should have listened to her husband's advice and not embarked on the trip. The other voice told her to accept the situation with a pinch of salt, and that before she knew it, she would be back at the palace with her beloved husband, and her disregard for his words would be long forgotten. After this continuous back and forth in her mind, the latter voice spoke again to reinforce the opinion that she would be back with her husband soon by reminding her that she was already travelling and would soon reach Ede to have some fun with her old friends. Adéníké knew, without a doubt, that the King's love for her was second to none. As soon as she remembered this, she smiled and focused once more on enjoying the journey.

The sky was now dark, and the Queen's envoy had approximately two more hours before they would arrive at Ede. Oláolú and the other three slaves rode closely behind the Queen's chariot, chatting away. Àlàní, who was well-known amongst the palace slaves and guards as a jester, had entertained them all the way. Oláolú always made sure to select Àlàní whenever he embarked on a journey because of his ability to liven up even the most boring of occasions. There was never a dull moment with Àlàní, and even a long journey would seem short with him on board.

As they rode through the last leg of the trip, Oláolú said to his friends, 'I know this may seem arbitrary, but I want to thank you, my friends, for coming with me on this trip to Ede. Thank you for being great friends and for being supportive.'

Túnjí responded, 'You are welcome, my friend. It is always my pleasure. You are very considerate, and

I am sure Àlàní and Gbadé would say the same about you, too.' Àlàní, who was sitting on the same horse as Túnjí, responded to his comment with long, hysterical laughter.

'What's so funny?' Oláolú and Gbadé asked.

'My fellow slave's response to Oláolú made me laugh,' said Àlàní. 'He responded as if he had the *choice* to say no when he is called upon to embark upon a duty for the Queen or the palace.' In a sarcastic tone, he added, 'When the master calls, you obey, my dear slave.'

'You are so dumb,' Túnjí retorted furiously. 'Everything is a joke to you. No one said that a slave should not obey his master. I was only appreciating Oláolú's comment.'

'You don't have to answer him,' said Oláolú. 'You know Àlàní will make a joke out of everything and anything. Someone who makes jokes about himself—what else did you expect?'

'I wasn't joking,' said Àlàní. 'I have a quick question for you guys: do any of you know the date we will retire from being slaves?' He laughed. 'Or do any of you know if slaves *get* to retire?'

'I am going to push you off this horse, Àlàní, if you don't stop asking dumb questions,' said Túnjí.

Gbadé, who was riding with Oláolú, jumped into the conversation. 'As dumb as the question sounds, I do think about it sometimes. I think about the day I can retire from working in the palace. Even if I cannot imagine a life outside the palace, the thought of it makes me excited.'

'You see?' said Àlàní. 'Someone here thinks like me. Master Túnjí, loyal slave—not everything I say is dumb.' He tickled Túnjí's side.

'Stop that, Àlàní!' Túnjí exclaimed. 'We will fall off the horse.'

The four men laughed as they continued riding behind the Queen's chariot.

After a few minutes of silence, Àlàní spoke again: 'My fellow slaves—'

Túnjí interrupted him. 'Could you please stop calling us your fellow slaves? Surely, you know our names.'

'Okay, I won't say that again. I am sorry, my fellow sla—friends. What I was going to say was that I am feeling very uncomfortable, and I need to poo. Oláolú, can you please get the attention of the guards in front and ask them to stop so I can drop this problem somewhere?'

Exasperated, Oláolú replied, 'We have less than two hours before reaching our destination. Can't you hold this problem inside until we arrive at Ede? You can see it is late, and I do not think it is advisable to stop here with the Queen, simply because a common slave wants to poo.'

Túnjí joined in again. 'After spending the last five hours saying only dumb things and rubbish, you want to drop some dumb shit now? Hmm?'

The men laughed.

'If you make me laugh any more, I will drop the poo on this horse.

'Seriously—please ask the guards to stop, only for a few minutes, or I will explode at any minute. I will not take long.'

Knowing Àlàní would not joke about such things, Oláolú agreed, and he alerted the guards leading the envoy who stopped, and Oláolú dismounted to inform Queen Adénìké of the reason why they had stopped.

Àlàní jumped off the horse, grabbed his water bottle, and ran into a nearby bush to relieve himself.

The entire envoy decided to use the opportunity to take a quick break. The guards made a fire and prepared to roast some corn they had brought along from the palace. The maidens and slaves sat around the fire with them as they turned and treated the corn to roast it evenly. Àlàní's impromptu respite turned out to be good for the crew, after all.

The Queen also stepped out of the chariot to stretch her legs after having held the same position for such a long period of time. As the Queen neared the chariot to board again, she walked to the back of the chariot, where she found Oláolú washing his face. His naked back and well-defined muscles shone in the light of the fire.

She drew close to him and touched his behind in a soft and ticklish manner.

Oláolú moved with reflex, bumping slightly against the unknown person. When he turned around to see who it was, he saw that it was the Queen, much to his surprise.

'Your Majesty...My Queen,' he said. 'I didn't...I wasn't...I am sorry...I didn't know you were standing there, My Queen.' He knelt on one knee and bowed his head in apology.

'Don't be sorry, Oláolú,' said Queen Adénìké. 'I was the one who touched you, and you are not at fault. I was pleased with what I saw, and thought to myself, why not feel it?'

He stared at her and gasped in amazement.

She smiled and continued. 'As you already know, the Queen is the mother of the kingdom and everything that resides inside it, both the living and the non-living, so I am your queen, and you belong to me. Get up!'

Oláolú rose from his kneeling position, his large and well-carved build emphasized in the glow. His physique almost overshadowed the Queen's. He looked at her reluctantly, and his gaze was met by her eyes, staring directly into his.

'I will need you like I always do when we arrive at Ede,' the Queen stated. 'And by the way, you may call me Adénìké, if you so wish.' She touched his cheek and massaged his neck all the way down to his chest before turning around and walking to get back into the chariot.

Oláolú wasn't surprised at her words. What surprised him was that the other crew members on the journey were only a stone's throw away from where the Queen had committed this act. He shook his head abruptly as though trying to awake from slumber, picked up the wash basin, and went straight to his travel pack to prepare to continue their journey. He also notified the envoy members who were eating and talking that the Queen was back in the chariot.

They finished eating and cleared the fire before returning to their places to resume the journey.

SEVEN

———◦•◦———

outh of the envoy in Ìkirè Kingdom was the home of the Basòrun, arguably the wealthiest man in the kingdom, excluding the royal family. His house lay on one-and-a-half acres of land and was the same house that his ancestors had lived in for close to two centuries. The Basòrun was well-respected in the kingdom. He has been successful at expanding the family business he'd inherited into other kingdoms, such as Oyo Kingdom. He had also begun establishing strong ties with the colonial masters trading cocoa.

The Basòrun paced around the dim fire in his yard. His wife and two sons sat around the fire watching him, waiting for the guard to return with his only daughter, Olúfúnké. The Basòrun was surprised not to find her at home when he'd arrived to discuss the decision he had made in the palace on the family's behalf. He had told his wife about his decision to marry off their only daughter to the King immediately. The Basòrun's family had always been close to the palace, but they secretly nursed the dream of ruling Ìkirè Kingdom one day. Just as he had told his wife, the Basòrun felt this would be a wonderful opportunity for his family to become a part of the royal lineage, and eventually, their future generations would take over the kingship.

Olúfúnké arrived with the guard a few minutes later. She had been at her boyfriend's house and was surprised that her father was home and wanted to see her. She was worried her father would scold her for not being at home when he'd arrived. To make matters worse, she had been at the house of a man who had not previously asked for her hand in marriage and at a very late hour in the evening. Still, the man with whom she had been spending time was not a stranger to the family, so she kept calm as she approached the yard where her parents and siblings were sitting and waiting. She expected to see her father alone, but when she saw her brothers and mother all sitting together quietly, her worries increased, and she hoped that nothing bad had happened.

She drew closer to her father and knelt down to greet him. '*Ekáalé baba mi* (good evening, my father),' she said.

'How are you, my darling daughter?' the Basòrun asked her.

'I am fine, sir,' answered Olúfúnké. 'I was at Olákúnlé's house, baba mi. He has not been feeling too well, so I took some food to him this evening.'

'That is fine. Take a seat, my daughter,' he instructed.

Olúfúnké got up from her kneeling position. Her worries about why her father had sent the guard to bring her home had been quieted, though she still wondered what it might be. Whatever it was, her family was there, so it should not be too bad, she thought as she approached and sat in the seat close to her mother. 'Good evening, *mama mi* (my mother).'

'Thank you, Olúfúnké,' her mother replied.

She sat close to her mother and waited patiently for her father to finish his discussion with the guard to tell them why he wanted to speak to them.

'My loving wife and children,' the Basòrun began. 'I know you are all wondering why I have returned from the meeting at the palace and requested your attention. The King brought a problem to the council this morning, and we have been weighing all possible options for a solution. As you all know, the King has no heir to inherit his throne, and this has caused him a lot of concern. After the priests consulted the gods, they were able to link the reason for the problem to an incident that happened in the palace a long time ago. Now, the only solution is a ritual that must be performed before sunrise tomorrow. Moreover, this ritual can only be performed by the King and a queen of our kingdom who is less than thirty-three years of age. Unfortunately, Queen Adénìké has travelled to Ede and cannot be brought back to the palace before sunrise, so the council has concluded the King must marry a new queen tonight, one with whom he can perform the ritual before sunrise and who may possibly bear the King's next heir to bring joy to the kingdom.'

The Basòrun paused to take a sip from the calabash of wine, brought to him by the guard while he'd been speaking.

'My loving family,' he continued, 'I see this as a great opportunity to fulfil the dreams of my forefathers and our family, and I have promised the King and council members that I would come home to speak with my family and bring back my daughter, Olúfúnké, to the palace to become the new queen of our great kingdom. Olúfúnké will also perform this ritual for which the palace and all of Ìkirè kingdom will be forever grateful.'

'But baba mi!' Olúfúnké cried out. 'Why would you suggest such a thing? I have someone I love and want to spend my life with. No, father, I will not accept this. I will not marry the King. Did you even think to ask me if I wanted to do this or not, baba mi?' She sobbed and fell down to the floor.

The Basòrun ignored his crying daughter and turned to address his wife. 'I must return with her to the palace in fifteen minutes. Speak to her and make her understand why it is important for her to do this. This is not about her nor me. These actions concern our family's past, present, and future. This is an order. The task is at hand, and she must perform the task. She should be proud, and I am proud of her already.

'We do not need to prepare anything for now, but if she is able to prepare her mind, she will be fine.

'I need to gather a few things, and I will be out shortly to take her to the palace.'

He turned back to his daughter and said gently, 'Olúfúnké, I am your father, and you can be rest assured that I will not open my eyes and watch something bad happen to you. You will be grateful to me for this one day.'

He signaled to his sons, who had been listening and watching in silence. They knew nothing about what was happening, but they surely knew enough about their father to understand that once he had made a decision, there was no going back.

Both sons stood to follow him as he walked into the house to gather what he needed before leaving for the palace with Olúfúnké.

King Adéorí was preparing to leave his chambers to return to the council room. Queen Adéòsun had left his chambers moments before. Adéorí had informed her about the recent developments at the council meeting and how he must marry a new wife to help perform the ritual rites as the priests had proposed. Adéòsun had been sad about the news, but she was especially unhappy because she had personally warned the younger queen, Adénìké, not to leave for her trip until the council meeting had concluded. Now, their husband would need to take a third wife which could certainly have been avoided. As a wise woman, she had understood the bigger picture and would support her husband so long as it would bring the cry of an heir and joy to the palace.

The situation seemed to transpire quickly. Adéorí took a few moments to think about the implications of marrying a new wife. The new woman he would bring to the palace was the Basòrun's daughter—a girl he also viewed as his own daughter. It all seemed unbelievable, but what could he do now? It was half-past midnight and very little time remained to make decisions or change decisions that had already been made. He also thought about his second wife, Adénìké, her trip to Ede, and how he had warned her not to leave. The situation would have been easier for both him and the palace if only she had listened to him.

The King stood up, said, '*Ibi líle latí ń bá okùnrin* (in the tough places are where we find a man),' and walked across his spacious room to the portrait of his late father, hanging on the wall. He knelt in front of the portrait and said a prayer, asking for guidance in this difficult time.

He rose and walked out of his room, full of renewed energy and courage. The three guards who were waiting at the door followed him as he strode from his chambers to the council room.

The King and the council members were all seated quietly when the Basòrun walked into the room with his daughter. Olúfúnké had been crying continuously from her father's house to the palace. It was difficult for her to come to terms with how things had changed for her in the blink of an eye. Her father made her wipe her tears before they stepped into the council room. Although she was no longer crying, her somber mood was apparent, and her eyes were red and heavy under the lights.

Her father bowed his head to the King and spoke briefly. 'Your Majesty, the ruler of our great kingdom and my fellow esteemed council members—thank you for your patience. I am here with my daughter, Olúfúnké, as promised. May Olódùmarè and the gods of our ancestors see us through this situation and many more to come.'

'Àse,' responded the council members.

'Thank you for your undiluted commitment to the throne and to our kingdom, Basòrun,' said King Adéorí. 'Only Olódùmarè has the capacity to reward you for what you have done and for your display of bravery. Please, you may take your seat.'

He then turned to speak to Olúfúnké. 'I understand this must have come as a shock to you—thank you for your understanding. You will forever remain a source of grace in our kingdom. Your courage will be continuously praised as a model for the children of our kingdom and our predecessors. Please, take your seat here,' the King directed, pointing to the chair immediately to his left.

Olúfúnké sat down quietly beside the King, still shocked and afraid. As soon as she'd sat down, the King glanced around the council room as though he were look-ing for something. After a moment he announced, 'We may proceed.'

The high priest stood to summon the guards to bring in the maidens who had been arranged for while the Basò-run was fetching his daughter. Four women entered the council room, each carrying a bowl containing honey, salt, bitter kola, and water. The high priest stepped towards them, said a few prayers, and asked the women to hand the bowls to Olúfúnké, one after the other, beginning with the bowl of bitter kola, then the salt, the honey, and the water. Olúfúnké was instructed by the high priest to take a bite of the kola, a lick of the salt, and a taste of the honey, feed the items to the King, and finally, drink from the bowl of water and share it with the King. After these things were done, the four maidens bowed their heads in front of the new queen to acknowledge her position before guiding her out of the council room to prepare her for the upcoming rites over the next few hours.

As she rose from her seat beside the King to go with the maidens, all council members—including her father—joyfully proclaimed, '*Olorì aya oba* (Queen and wife of the King)!'

The early morning hours approached quickly. The cocks began to crow their first rounds for the day. The priests had prepared everything for the ritual through the night due to the limited amount of time available to get all the items ready. The King had also remained awake throughout the night, and he was now out of his chambers and ready to go. The maidens readied the new queen, and they were prepared to set out for the Òsun River.

Everything had happened so fast for the new queen that she was still trying to come to terms with her new reality. The maidens took her to the council room where the initial commencement of scheduled rites would begin before going to the Òsun River with the King, the eight priests, and some guards.

Just before Olúfúnké and the maidens entered the council room, Queen Adéòsun—escorted by two guards—came through to offer greetings, words of support, and to wish Olúfúnké well for the day.

The maidens and guards bowed to Queen Adéòsun as she approached Olúfúnké.

The new queen rose from her seat, then knelt down to greet and acknowledge Queen Adéòsun, whom she had always seen as a role model and mother of the kingdom.

'Stand up, My Queen,' Adéòsun said to Olúfúnké. 'I am here for you, Olúfúnké, and will *always* be here to support you. Thank you for your understanding and for your assistance in this situation. You are now our family and will always be a part of our family.'

Olúfúnké replied, 'Thank you, ma. Your presence here this morning means a lot to me and makes me feel stronger. Thank you, My Queen.'

The high priest came out of the council room to invite Queen Olúfúnké inside. She spent five minutes behind closed doors with the priests and the King before the doors were opened and they set out for the Òsun River.

EIGHT

———•◦•———

Queen Adénìké's visit to Ede proceeded smoothly. The Queen and her friends truly made the most of their time together and engaged in plenty of fun activities. The guards, slaves, and maidens spent their time eating, relaxing, and playing games while accompanying the Queen. Aside from the long and stressful ride to Ede, they considered the trip a holiday away from the palace, and they tried to make the very best of it. The entourage stayed at Foláshadé's compound. Foláshadé, Adénìké's childhood friend and best friend of eighteen years, had moved to Ede when she'd married her husband, who was one of Ede's wealthiest men. Foláshadé's house was big enough to accommodate both her friends and Adénìké's entourage comfortably. Nothing gave Foláshadé more joy than to host her three dearest friends at her house, and the past few days had been very fulfilling for her.

On the last night of the Queen's visit, she made plans to return to Ìkirè the next morning. Dinner was served by

Foláshadé's maids and throughout the vacation, the four friends had always eaten their meals together, but on that evening, Adénìké had not yet joined them, though the maids had gone to inform the Queen fifteen minutes ahead of time that dinner was about to be served. When dinner was eventually served, Adénìké had not yet made her appearance.

Foláshadé and her friends began idle conversation with the hope Adénìké would join them shortly, and they could all eat together as before. As this was their last night together before Adénìké left, it couldn't have been more important.

Finally, one of the women decided to speak about it: 'Our *iyán* (pounded yam) and *ègúsí* (melon soup) is getting cold,' said Jùmòké. 'Where is Adénìké? Are you girls sure we should not begin eating without her? She can join us when she is ready.'

Omololá responded, 'Yes, our food is definitely getting cold. I wonder what is keeping Adénìké so long? I know her people are getting ready for their journey back to Ìkirè, but she obviously would not be doing any of the packing. I hope she is all right.'

'That's what I was thinking, too,' Foláshadé agreed. 'I hope everything is okay with her. You girls know that she can be very sensitive—I hope no one has pissed her off.'

Jùmòké added, 'Well, I think we should eat, and she can join us later. Or better still, the maids could bring her something fresh when she arrives. If not, we won't be able to enjoy this food that had such a wonderful aroma because of her.'

Then, Foláshadé said, 'Girls, let me go and check on her quickly. If she is not ready, at least I will be able to confirm, or I might bring her with me. Hopefully, it's nothing serious.'

'That's a good idea, Foláshadé,' Omololá commented. 'We will wait for you. Please tell her to hurry up because some people out here are hungry.' The girls laughed as Foláshadé got up to check on Adénìké.

Foláshadé's compound was not as big as the King's palace in Ìkirè, of course, but it was larger than the average compound in Ede or its neighbouring cities. The building that had been prepared for Adénìké and her entourage had been built specifically for high-profile guests.

As Foláshadé headed towards Adénìké's room, she decided to walk past the dining area to see if Adénìké's entourage had begun eating yet and if Adénìké was there. The entourage was eating and chatting away, but she saw no sign of Adénìké.

The entourage paused to greet her. She returned their greeting and continued to Adéníké's room, walking along the long corridor leading to the guestroom occupied by the Queen. As she approached, she heard Adénìké's soft voice. As she drew closer, the intent of the words became clearer. To her wildest surprise, Adénìké was speaking quietly to someone else in the room, while responding with pleasure.

Foláshadé's heart skipped a beat as she stood in front of the door. What she had heard with her ears and what she wanted to believe in her heart were two very different things.

She heard a man's subdued voice saying, 'You are so beautiful, Adéníké,' as Adéníké continued to moan with pleasure.

Foláshadé felt as if her heart had almost jumped out of her mouth. She was amazed, confused, and disturbed all at once. For a split second, she wondered who the man was. Her husband was away on a trip of his own, or she might have suspected him as the man with Adéníké. She thought about barging into the room to see who it was, but she held herself back and decided to wait outside to see who would come out with Adéníké.

She thought about the King of Ìkirè, a man she respected so much, and her eyes teared up, knowing that her friend was committing a huge blunder. It was an atrocity that was bound to be exposed sooner or later.

Barely five minutes after Foláshadé had left the guest building, as she waited patiently by a guava tree in the corner where she would be unnoticed, the man who had been satisfying her friend, the Queen, appeared.

Without realizing it, Foláshadé exclaimed, 'Olórun mi! (my God)' out loud, and she watched as the man walked towards the entourage's dining area. Blinking rapidly to keep from crying, she contemplated whether to return to her friends at the table or to meet Adéníké and confront her about what she had just heard and seen. She decided to go to Adénìké's room to confront her immediately to hear what she had to say about this abomination.

As Foláshadé approached the room again, a part of her felt as if she were dreaming and might possibly wake up soon to realize that none of it had been real.

She went to the door and knocked twice.

From the other side, Adénìké called out, 'Who is there?'

'It's me: Foláshadé. May I come in?'

'Yes, please, come in,' answered Adénìké.

Foláshadé opened the door to see her friend getting dressed.

'*Báwo ni Òré mi* (how are you, my friend)?' the Queen asked. 'You should not be knocking to enter a room in your own house, my dear friend.' The Queen smiled.

'I must knock first, Adénìké, because a Queen is in the room, and one could not know what the Queen might be up to. One cannot just invade her privacy.'

'You make me laugh with the queen courtesy. I am your friend first before I am the queen. Please, always remember that. I am also late for dinner. I know you and the girls must have wondered why I took so long, but I dozed off while waiting and woke up only a few minutes ago. I am sorry about that. I guess I was just tired.'

'That's fine,' said Foláshadé. 'We did wonder about it, so I thought I would come to check on you. I have been at your door for about fifteen minutes, but I figured you were busy with someone, so I decided to wait until you were done before coming in.'

Adénìké looked at her friend with amazement and some shame after hearing those words, and she did not know how to react. She wondered what Foláshadé might know, what she had seen, or if she had, indeed, seen anything at all, but before she could come to any meaningful conclusions, Foláshadé continued.

'Adénìké, you are sleeping with Oláolú, a palace slave. I saw and heard everything, so don't try to say otherwise. Just tell me the truth. How long has this been going on? Why are you doing this? What happens if the King learns about this?' Foláshadé had so many questions, they kept coming one after the other, even before Adénìké could answer any of them.

Adénìké kept silent as her eyes filled with tears. Her secret had finally been revealed to her closest friend.

'Answer me, Adénìké!' Foláshadé demanded. 'Who am I to judge you or your actions, but don't you realize that it is a huge taboo? Did you ever think of how King Adéorí would feel or what he might do if he ever found out about this? You know how powerful your husband is, and you dare to do this…in my house! Do you want to bring me trouble? Don't you realize that if either of our husbands ever found out, they would say I was supporting it, and that you come to my home to sleep with men?

'At any rate, we will discuss this after dinner. I do not want the girls to know anything about this mess you have created for yourself yet. Get dressed and meet me in the dining hall. We have been waiting for you.'

Foláshadé left the room immediately without waiting for Adénìké's response, shutting the door behind her with a mixture of disgust, fear, and anger.

Queen Adénìké was dumbfounded. Her best friend now knew the secret she had been keeping for months. Her friend's words had cut deeply. Tears flowed, trickling down her face as she sat in the guestroom, not knowing what to do next. She knew that she had been lucky that Foláshadé had been the one to find out, as it could well have been someone else.

She remembered Foláshadé's last few words, telling her to join them for dinner, and she braced herself and finished dressing, trying to hide the anguish in her expression. She knew behaving in a manner that would raise the suspicion of her two other friends or the staff would only make things worse.

As she left the room, she wondered if Oláolú had seen Foláshadé or suspected that she knew their secret.

The girls finished eating their dinner, which had been wonderful, as expected. At that point, their wait for Adénìké was inconsequential. The maids cleared the plates, and Foláshadé ordered palm wine to be served as they relaxed to enjoy the rest of their final evening together. Although Adénìké had done a pretty good job of keeping the mood and conversation going, when she had made eye contact with Foláshadé a few times, she could see that her friend was not happy about what she had caught the Queen doing.

The wine was served, and the girls continued chatting, two of them still unaware of what had ensued between Foláshadé and Adénìké earlier.

Jùmòké, the chattiest and wittiest of the girls, was the first to stir up the conversation. Speaking to the maid serving the palm wine, she commented, 'Oh, my goodness—this wine tastes so good, just like the pounded yam and ègúsí soup. I have never eaten yams pounded so well and fine without any *kókó* (lumps) in it. Was it you that pounded the yam?' she asked. 'Or did you ask one of Adénìké's slave boys to do the pounding? One of them looks really strong, and I imagine that his pounded yam would be sooo soft.'

Omololá looked amused at Jùmòké's comment, assuming she had only been joking, but at the same time, knowing she usually had a reason for saying those kinds of things.

'No,' answered the maid, shocked. 'We pounded the yam ourselves, ma. I and the other maids.'

'Don't mind her,' Omololá said to the maid. 'She is only pulling your leg. Although I do agree that you did a fine job with the food.'

She then turned to Jùmòké. 'Aunty Jùmòké, what do you mean, 'one of Adénìké's slaves looks very strong,' hmm? Have you begun eyeing one of the boys now? I wouldn't be surprised,' Omololá said sarcastically, with a smile.

'Yes,' replied Jùmòké. 'I mean, one of Adénìké's slaves is very strong, physically, and I must say, he looks good, too. I am sure Adénìké knows the one I am talking about, after all, they all work for her, and she would know their capabilities, right, Adénìké?'

Adénìké felt extremely uncomfortable when her eyes met Foláshadé's again for what must have been the tenth time. Her discomfort was obvious from her expression, and Jùmòké noticed it almost immediately, even though she'd expected her friend to consider her question as a joke.

'Jùmòké,' Foláshadé said, 'only you would know who was strong and who could pound yams better.'

'Maybe you *are* eyeing one of the slaves,' Omololá said to Jùmòké. 'Who knows? Tell us, so Adénìké can introduce him to you.'

The girls laughed playfully. Adénìké managed to join in with them, but deep down, she was confused. She wondered if the conversation were a coincidence or if Jùmòké and Omololá knew something about her affair, too. She became lost in her thoughts for a few moments, but then, reassured herself that, of course, she could trust Foláshadé completely.

The conversation carried on, and the girls enjoyed their wine and talked about other things as the night grew darker.

NINE

Night turned into morning very quickly in Ede. The entourage had started preparing for the journey back to Ìkirè. The past six days had been relaxing for the crew. Everyone in the entourage loved Queen Adénìké because of her easygoing nature, and they were always glad to embark on such trips with her. The maidens and slaves were loading the carriage while the guards fed and readied the horses, and they planned to set out by eight o'clock, within the next thirty minutes.

The previous night, the girls had agreed to meet in Adénìké's room to say goodbye and wish her a safe trip before she set out for home. At that time, Adénìké was sitting alone in the room, dressed and ready, sipping her morning *àgbo* (herbal tea), and staring out the window, watching the birds as they sang and perched on the trees. Foláshadé was the first of her friends to arrive. As soon as she opened the door and walked in, Adénìké rose, hugged her tightly, and began to cry profusely.

'Come on, 'Dénìké,' Foláshadé said fondly, 'don't beat yourself up so badly.' From one look at Adénìké's puffy eyes, it was obvious to see that she'd had little to no sleep the previous night.

Adénìké tried to stop the tears, but she could not. 'I feel so terrible and confused. I can't believe that I failed to realize the magnitude of what I was doing before you forced me to see it. I am so afraid. The King does not know about this, but I don't know if I will be able to look him in the eye when I see him.'

'Wipe your tears first because Jùmòké and Omololá will be here soon, and I do not think you will want to explain anything to them right now,' Foláshadé admonished, using the corner of the wrapper tied around her waist to wipe the tears from Adénìké's cheeks. 'Now, my only advice for you is to desist from this act. I discovered it, and you can never be too sure who will find out next. As much as I do not want to be a part of this, whatever concerns you concerns me, too, and you know that all I want is the best for you. Go back home, let this be the last time you ever see that boy again, and make sure you keep your mouth shut about it. Your secret is safe with me. I am sure you know that.'

Adénìké hugged her friend again. She knew she could always count on Foláshadé. She was the only person in the entire world whom she trusted wholeheartedly, and Adénìké considered her the sister she'd never had. Folá-shadé's home had always been a place of comfort and peace for her. Both ladies walked out of the room to meet

Jùmòké and Omololá, who were just outside, chatting away with Adénìké's maidens.

'We should do this again sometime soon, Adénìké. Thank you for blessing us with your presence, Your Majesty,' Omololá said with a smile, as she bowed her head in respect to her friend. Jùmòké bowed her head also, mimicking Omololá, and all four friends laughed.

'Yes, it is always my pleasure,' replied Adénìké. 'And we are definitely doing this again very soon. Even my entourage loves it here. The only problem is that my husband will want you to come to the palace to spend some time with us the next time. So, I am taking this opportunity to invite you all to the palace officially. Just let me know when you are ready, and we will make preparations.'

'Yaaaaay! Now, I am looking forward to that,' Jùmòké said, cheerfully. Turning to Foláshadé, she added, 'Not that I didn't enjoy being at this beautiful house and compound of yours, Foláshadé, but you know that visiting the great palace of Ìkirè is always *exceptional*.' Her naughty smile spoke volumes.

'Ha-ha, Jùmòké,' said Omololá. 'Must you say everything that comes to mind?'

'Yes, I must,' she answered, with a devious expression.

The girls laughed again and came together for one big hug. Overall, their time together had been wonderful. Adénìké's guards, slaves, and maidens thanked Foláshadé for her kindness and hospitality, and the maidens helped Queen Adénìké step into the carriage. Foláshadé, Jùmòké, and Omololá waved goodbye as Queen Adénìké and her entourage slowly and majestically proceeded out of Foláshadé's compound to begin their journey home.

Compared to the last few days, many fewer activities seemed to be taking place at King Adéorí's palace. The end-of-year festival, the council meeting, the King's marriage to a new wife, and the performance of the ritual, had been very demanding for the King and the palace as a whole. As the common adage says, 'Problems come, and problems go,' whether they are tackled or not, but those who tackle their problems are the ones who come out of them victorious. The King and his council members showed a high level of resilience and wisdom in tackling the problem faced by the palace without raising much alarm amongst the people in the kingdom. The ritual performed by the new queen went well and had been marked as a success.

The news about Olúfúnké becoming the new queen had spread throughout the kingdom with mixed reactions from Ìkirè's people. Some people deduced that the King had married her due to the need to produce an heir while others were skeptical and believed there must have been ongoing issues between the King and the queens for him to have taken another wife overnight. The majority of the people also knew that their ruler was highly intelligent and didn't make frivolous decisions. They viewed the King's decisions with the highest level of trust, and it was business as usual—whatever anyone thought or believed, the King's decisions were always final, and the people had to live with them either way.

The new queen spent quite a bit of time with the King after the ritual, as expected. She was settling into her new role and home as the new queen of Ìkirè Kingdom. Five days after her father had first suggested she marry the King, her life still felt like a dream to her, although the reality dawned on her more and more as the days passed. Olúfúnké was particularly grateful to Queen Adéòsun, who had been extremely kind and accommodating to her, but she still wondered how Queen Adénìké would react to the news upon her return from Ede. Olúfúnké knew that because Adénìké was younger than Adéòsun, she might see the situation in a different light, but the fact still remained that Olúfúnké had been officially married into the palace, and nothing could change that, certainly not after having performed the rituals to save the palace from its barren state.

She was beginning to look forward to the grand marriage ceremony to the King, which was slated to take place in four weeks, on the first weekend of the coming month. Guests and allies of Ìkirè Kingdom from neighbouring and distant lands would be present to grace the occasion. The priests had advised her to spend the seven days after the ritual alone with the King, who had given the orders to renovate one of the palace's unoccupied properties, to be converted into Olúfúnké's private chambers. As spontaneous and quick as everything seemed to be happening in her eyes, the experience might even surpass that of which she had always dreamed. Thoughts of the man with whom she had previously spent most of her time and with whom she had hoped to spend her life crossed her mind from time to time, but the prospects of a great future and how she might use her new position to affect lives were now staring her in the face. The thought of being the woman who would give the great King Adéorí an heir made her ecstatic, and the hate she'd felt for her father when he'd initially proposed that she marry the King was slowly turned back to love, and faster than she'd imagined.

That same evening at half-past five, Queen Adénìké arrived back at the palace with her entourage. They were very tired as they'd stopped only once on the journey back from Ede. The Queen had been adamant about reaching Ìkirè before sunset, so the guards had considered it important to do so. The King preferred that the queens travelled during the daytime and had, on a few occasions, expressed great dissatisfaction when a queen had not tried to avoid nighttime travel. Upon her arrival, Queen Adénìké was welcomed by maidens and guards, who decorated her path with flowers and incense. The sound of drums and flutes added a royal grandeur to the Queen's welcome.

The guards helped Adénìké step down from the chariot. Many maidens greeted her briefly, and she went almost immediately to her chambers. Her worry had only increased since the incident in Ede the night before. She continued to feel dreadful, as if she had betrayed the King's trust in her. She also wondered if she could bear the King's reaction if he ever found out.Once in her private chambers, she disrobed and took a warm bath that had been prepared for her upon arrival. Her skin appeared dry from the long journey, so she applied some oil. Then, she donned one of her finest dresses and headed for the King's chambers.

The King was in the chambers' common room, chatting with Queen Olúfúnké. He had spent most of his free time with her since the ritual. She had stayed in the King's private chambers until that morning because she had been required to not see anyone other than the King until the seventh day after the ritual. That day was the first day she was allowed to see other people after the ritual as Queen of Ìkìrè Kingdom. King Adéorí had kept her company and used the opportunity to get to know her further. Despite their age gap of more than thirty years, the two got along fairly well. The guards had informed the King of Queen Adénìké's arrival, and he had expected her to come to his chambers at any moment, as she usually did after her long trips.Adénìké walked into the common room, excited to see her husband. No one had told her the news about the new queen in the palace yet. On her way in from Ede, she'd noticed movement in the direction of ongoing construction in the palace, but she had no idea that they were building the new queen's chambers. The King had promised Adénìké when they'd married that she would be his second and last wife. She also knew that the King loved her dearly, and taking another wife would be the last thing on his mind, so she would never have imagined this would be the case. She saw King Adéorí sitting on his throne in the palace's common room and noticed a beautiful, elegantly dressed young woman beside him. Adénìké recognized the woman as the Basòrun's daughter, and her first instinct was that she had come to visit the King. She approached the throne and knelt down before her husband to greet him.

'*Ekú ilé olówó orí mi* (greetings to the owner and payer of my bride price),' said Queen Adénìké. 'I have missed you so much.' She leaned forward from her kneeling position to hug the King, and he patted her back with his hands.

'*Kú àbò Aya Oba* (welcome back, wife of the King). I hope you returned in peace. How was your holiday, and how were your friends?'

'It went well, My Lord. My friends, especially Foláshadé, send their warm greetings to you, my husband. I extended your invitation to them, and they will be visiting us sometime soon,' she said, smiling.

During their conversation, Olúfúnké sat quietly, watching and listening. Adénìké turned to Olúfúnké and asked, 'How are you, dear? And how is your father?'

'I'm doing well, My Queen. My father is also doing well,' she answered.

King Adéorí asked Olúfúnké to excuse them, so she stood up and went into the King's inner chambers. Adénìké was surprised to see Olúfúnké enter the inner chambers, but she assumed the King would have an explanation. As soon as the younger woman was out of sight, Adéorí asked Adénìké to sit beside him. From the expression on his face, she could see that something was weighing on his mind.

'*Igi gogoro má gùn mi lójú, àti òkèrè latí ń wó bò* (the pointed stick that will pierce one in the eye is avoided while it is still far off),' King Adéorí began.

At these words, Adénìké became confused, and her heart beat faster. She wondered if the King was still upset about her leaving on the journey to Ede, and she paid careful attention when King Adéorí continued.

'I warned you not to leave this palace until the meeting with the council of elders was concluded, but as usual, you refused and flagrantly disobeyed my orders in my own palace, in my own kingdom. The meeting with the council of elders was concluded the same night you left for Ede. *Ó ye kí o mò wípé sùúrù lérè* (You should know that patience is a virtue). The council members completed their findings and came to a decision about the issue that warranted the meeting in the first place. The decision and solution to resolve the matter required that an old, incomplete ritual performed by my ancestors be completed in order for an heir who will inherit my throne to be born into the palace. The requirements for the ritual stipulated that a queen of my kingdom, not older than thirty-three years of age, go with me to the Òsun River and complete the cleansing. Moreover, this incomplete ritual had to be performed before the next day's sunrise.'

By this point, Adénìké was even more confused as she attempted to digest her husband's words. She realised she'd crossed the line this time, but she still could not fathom how much damage she had done.

'As you may have already guessed,' the King continued, 'you were the only queen who fit the requirements for the ritual perfectly, but because of your disrespect for the throne in favour of frivolous worldly things, you were nowhere to be found. And since Adéòsun did not fit the requirements, I had no choice but to marry Olúfúnké that same night, so she could perform the ritual with me. This happened, of course, with the consent of Adéòsun and the members of my council. As you know, the issue of producing an heir is of highest priority to the palace, and that is why you now see Olúfúnké in the palace, and she is here to stay, as my new queen.'

Uncontrollable tears poured from Adénìké's eyes. She could not believe what she had just heard. She would never, in a thousand years, have believed this could happen; and even if it could, not in such a manner. One of her biggest fears had materialised, and she felt like screaming out loud, but she knew that her disobedience to the crown had cost her more this time than she'd ever thought possible.

King Adéorí said gently, '*Mo ní ìfé re gidi gan* (I love you very much), Adénìké, and I know that you know this, but we have to accept this the way it has come about and work together to make the best out of the situation.' Not minding whether she had something to say or not, the King called Olúfúnké back into the common room before Adénìké could respond.Olúfúnké had been worried about how Queen Adénìké would react to the news, but she also knew that the King's words were the law, and his decisions and actions were final. She walked into the common room quietly. Adénìké, who had buried her face in her palms and was weeping profusely, lifted her head to see the face of the new queen of the kingdom.

Addressing Adénìké, Adéorí said, 'I am sure you know, Olúfúnké, the Basòrun's daughter. She will be your *ìyàwó* (junior wife). Please, kindly welcome her to the palace with all your love and support because she is now one of us.'

Adénìké could no longer hold back her frustration and misery, and she fell to the floor, sobbing.

The King patted her back a few times, saying, 'Adénìké, this could have been very different. *Nkan tí àgbàlagbà ńrí tí o bá jòkó sí abé igi òpe, omodé o le ri tí óbá gun orí igi òpe kań nà* (what an elder sees from merely sitting at the bottom of a palm tree, a child cannot see even if they climb to the top of the palm tree).' Adéorí was also unhappy with the situation. He stood from the throne, and he and Olúfúnké entered his inner chambers together.

Adénìké remained on the floor, blaming herself as she continued to weep. She felt as if she were trapped in a terrible, unbelievable dream. After a time, she forced herself to get up and leave for her chambers. She believed the day was probably the saddest of her entire life.

TEN

Ten days after the yearly farm harvest festival had concluded, the palace was enjoying a calm break with flexible schedules for guards and slaves alike. Aside from the guards who were monitoring the ongoing construction of Queen Olúfúnké's chambers, the staff's mood was fairly relaxed.

At 5:30pm on that warm and serene Thursday evening, Oláolú and some of the other contestants were practising on the palace's field for the upcoming pankration tournament. When the preliminaries for the contest were over, sixteen slaves had been selected to participate in the final contest, scheduled to take place in the palace square the coming weekend, beginning the next day, which was Friday. The tournament was expected to last through Sunday with the semi-finals slated for Saturday and finals for Sunday. Oláolú had returned to his training since he had missed out on participating in the preliminaries because of the journey to Ede with Queen

Adénìké. As the previous winner, he automatically qualified for that year's contest, and expectations for him were high. By far the best fighter in the kingdom, everyone—including the other contestants—expected nothing short of a victory from him.

Aside from the joy and respect that would come from achieving victory in the age-old palace tradition, he also desired to retain his title as *Alágbára lárìn erú,* so he could continue to enjoy all the benefits that came with it, such as a larger palace dorm residence and flexible schedule. The only true contender of which Oláolú was aware in that year's contest was Olúgbénró, the third runner-up from last year, whom he'd defeated in the previous semi-finals. Most of those who had witnessed the semi-final match between Oláolú and Olúgbénró had declared it the best pankration fight they had ever seen, while others had viewed it as the final match.

Olúgbénró, who had been practising very hard for that year's contest, had won all of his preliminary matches with near-flawless victories. Fans and citizens of the kingdom patiently anticipated the start of the tournament on Friday, and many predicted it would be Oláolú versus Olúgbénró in the final match.

As soon as Oláolú took a break from his practise to rest, his friend, Àlàní, walked up to him to tap him on the shoulder. '*Alágbára* (the powerful),' Àlàní said jokingly as he sat down beside him.

'How is it going, Àlàní?' greeted Oláolú. 'I hope you have brought good news this time because I know you like to speak about everything you see, *elènu màrí màso* (the one whose mouth says everything that is seen).'

'You're not serious, Oláolú. Later, you will say I talk too much. Are you not the one who has started calling me names now, Mr Alágbára?'

'Okay, sorry—you know I am only telling the truth. You make it sound as if I have called you someone you are not.

'In any case, how are you today? I know you do not have the power to fight. You only have the power to talk. So, what do you have for me, because I will be back on the field in five minutes?' He looked at Àlàní expectantly.

'Haba Oláolú, your mouth is fast and sharp today. You are just throwing shade at me, but since I am your number one fan, and I want you to win the tournament on Sunday, I will consider your insults as a part of your practise. I am sure you are training your speech, so it is sharp enough to use against your opponents in the matches.' Both men laughed.

'Well, I just came over here to give you some words of encouragement, Alágbára,' said Àlàní. He hesitated for a moment. 'I have not seen much of Queen Adénìké since we returned from Ede. I heard that she'd locked herself in her chambers for four days after we arrived. I was just wondering why she would do that. And since you are her most loved slave, I thought you might have some idea what is going on with her.'

'Àlàní, you are going to kill me. I knew it wasn't possible for you to come in peace without bringing some news.

Oh, well. Do you see that pathway?' Oláolú pointed in the direction of the palace's chambers area.

'Yes, I do,' Àlàní responded, 'and what do I do with that?'

'Good. Walk down that path, turn left, and keep walking. The last building on the right is Queen Adénìké's chambers. Go in and ask her why she has not come out of her chambers for four days. I am sure that is where you will find the best answer.'

'I can't even believe the garbage I was just listening to—I am serious, Oláolú! I am just worried about the Queen. She is always very lively, and up until we arrived at the palace, nothing seemed to be wrong with her. I think something must have happened to make her sad.' Àlàní thought for a moment, then exclaimed, 'Oh, oh, oh—now I think I might have a clue. Maybe it was because the King married a new wife while we were away, and she hid herself for four days in protest.'

'You are a clown, Àlàní. So, you were aware of these possibilities before you came to ask me this silly question, hmm? Yes, I think she *was* protesting. I am sure you must have seen all of the maids from Queen Adénìké's chambers joining together to voice their disapproval of the new queen in front of the King's chambers.' Oláolú hissed through his teeth and stood up. 'I must continue training now. I will see you later this evening with the guys. You can sit here and wait for my response to your question, or better still, you can go join the maids in their protest, you joker,' he said, laughing, as he walked off towards the practise field.

'I was only concerned, Mr Alágbára,' Àlàní yelled after him. He smiled, shook his head, stood up, and walked off in the opposite direction.

On Sunday, the final match was scheduled to begin by 5:00 p.m. The day had turned out to be very interesting and colourful as every citizen of the kingdom looked for-wards to this year's final match. On Friday and Saturday, onlookers were entertained by many highlights during the opening rounds of matches and knock-out stages. Visitors from neighbouring kingdoms were also present to enjoy the thrilling weekend in Ìkirè. Kings, queens, chiefs, and elders from those kingdoms were not left out of what could be called one of the most anticipated pan-kration fights in the region. Plenty of food and drink were available to all in attendance. Young and old placed high-stakes bets on the outcomes of matches, and the atmo-sphere in the kingdom was especially lively.

One of the main highlights of Saturday's semi-finals was the match between Olúgbénró—the closest title con-tender—and Ifárìndé—one of the fastest-rising fighters in the kingdom. Ifárìndé, who had been impressive enough to win his first two matches, was knocked out in less than two minutes and had to be taken for immediate treatment by the palace guards. In the semi-final rounds, fights usually lasted about twenty to thirty minutes. Olúgbénró had won the last match on Saturday, which placed him in the final round of the tournament for the first time. He was set to face the top fighter of the kingdom—Oláolú—who had won a tightly contested match against Olágbagi in the semi-finals.

Predictions for the Oláolú versus Olúgbénró final were made. All over the kingdom, everyone talked about the much-awaited match between the two talented slaves. The hopes of Olúgbénró's fans had grown because of his swift, impressive victory in his last match, accompanied by his flawless performance, and men and women all over the kingdom placed high-stakes bets on the outcome.

King Adéorí and all the dignitaries present were seated at the high table in the executive corner, waiting for the two contestants to step onto the field. An overwhelmingly large crowd of citizens and onlookers were present. The three queens were also seated next to the King, with Adéòsun in the seat closest to him. Queen Adénìké had been quiet for most of the week, but she seemed happy to be present to witness the glamour and excitement of the day. She was still very sad, but she was heartened to see her dear Oláolú in the finals for the third year in a row.

A loud roar of excitement went up from the crowd as the two fighters walked through the throng of people and approached the field. The two referees who would manage the match walked behind them as the fans shouted at the top of their voices. This moment was surely much anticipated. Besides the title, the egos of both men were also at stake. Olúgbénró was tired of standing in Oláolú's shadow, the man who had defeated him in the semi-finals the previous year. For Oláolú, nothing would be worse than to be defeated by an opponent whom he'd watched progress and whom everyone clearly saw as an inferior fighter by comparison. Olúgbénró's rapid win the day before had gained him merit as a solid contender for the title in people's eyes.

The cheering subsided as King Adéorí stood to commence the final match. The two competitors were ready to battle, and in less than thirty minutes, the new winner of that year's tournament would be announced.

The referee blew the whistle, and the match began.

Both men circled the field, and the cheering from the crowd increased. They appeared to be evenly matched. As expected by most who tried to analyse the match-up, Olúgbénró controlled the first ten minutes of the fight, almost taking Oláolú down in the ninth minute with a jab to the left eye.

Oláolú's eyelid began to bleed. The bleeding became more profuse, and the referee stopped the fight in the fifteenth minute for Oláolú to have his eyelid cleaned to prevent the blood from blocking his vision. Oláolú's anger grew with the sight of his blood when the field aides treated him. The bleeding diminished, and he got back onto the field to continue the fight with the crowd cheering him on.

Oláolú was convinced that he needed to gain full control of the situation. Olúgbénró had the upper-hand and would know that he had to focus on Oláolú's left eye, which was already injured. As long as he continued to be rough and get shots at the cut eye, he would weaken Oláolú and have a greater chance of knocking him out.

The match continued, and to the shock of the crowd— and some of Olúgbénró's fans, the tables turned very quickly. Barely two minutes after the fight had resumed, Oláolú successfully lifted Olúgbénró up and slammed him, face down, on the floor. This move was unique to Oláolú, and the crowd went wild.

Olúgbénró screamed out in pain.

Oláolú had won competitions in the past with this same move. It was one that opponents feared. For this move, he lifted up his opponent and laid his opponent's stomach across both shoulders behind his neck. Then, he threw him facedown, flat on the sand, while moving out of the way. Most opponents on whom Oláolú had suc- cessfully made this move passed out immediately.

The fans waited patiently as Olúgbénró moaned in pain, rolling from left to right on the ground as he held his palms to his face. There was blood on his face and palms, meaning he was obviously injured. Olúgbénró's nose had been broken, but he managed to get up to his feet about thirty seconds later, and the crowd chanted loudly again.

Oláolú knew the time had come to finish the match. As soon as the referee gave the go-ahead to continue, he rushed forward and jabbed Olúgbénró thrice in the lower ribs—left, right, and then left again—with his renowned combination.

Olúgbénró immediately guarded his ribs with his hands, leaving his upper region, neck, and face exposed for Oláolú to take advantage of.

In the blink of an eye, Oláolú grabbed the other fighter's neck and slammed Olúgbénró's face and broken nose against his shoulder with another fancy move.

Olúgbénró fell to the floor again, lifeless.

The crowd went into another frenzy of screams. The King, queens, and guests were amazed at Oláolú's superior skill and talent. No one had ever witnessed anything like that before, anywhere in the kingdom.

Queen Adénìké's face was all smiles, and everyone could tell that the final match was coming to an end.

Oláolú bellowed and hit his chest numerous times to show his strength as he faced the crowd. He walked over to Olúgbénró's motionless body and placed his foot on his chest. The referee waited for another thirty seconds, but there was no sign of movement from Olúgbénró. After twenty-seven minutes of fighting, Oláolú was declared the winner of the tournament for the third, consecutive year.

The field aides arrived quickly to take Olúgbénró away for treatment. By that point, some of his fans had joined Oláolú on the field as he was cheered and praised by everyone. The fight had, indeed, been one of a kind. Oláolú was excited, but he also understood that Olúgbénró had been a strong force with which to reckon.

After about fifteen minutes of jubilation, the crowd, fans, and people of Ìkirè Kingdom settled down for the closing ceremonies in which the King would bestow the title of Alágbára Lárìń Àwon Erú on the winner and present him with awards.

Oláolú walked out from the crowd. His fans were ecstatic, and their noise filled the entire palace. Hearing the fans express their joy gave him goosebumps all over. He knew he'd just fought a strong opponent in the longest ever final tournament fight. He walked towards the high table and knelt in front of King Adéorí. Other attending rulers also waved their *ìrùkèrè* (fly whisks made of horsehair strands fastened to a stick by a leather handle) to show their affirmation. The King then placed a golden necklace around Oláolú's neck and patted his back with his ìrùkèrè.

The crowd shouted jubilantly in response, and King Adéorí announced that it was time for the final part of the closing ceremonies. The drummers beat their drums, and music flowed from the instruments in a wonderful symphony. The night progressed with abundant food, drink, and dance. In the history of the palace's pankration tradition, surely this was a night that Oláolú, Olúgbénró, and the entire Ìkirè Kingdom would remember for a very long time.

ELEVEN

———————— ••• ————————

Six weeks after the yearly pankration tournament, it was also six weeks into the new farming season. As usual, crops were being traded daily in the market, and preparation for planting had begun. The builders had completed the new queen's chambers, and she had moved in. Palace guards had been reshuffled, the season had started with much hope for the future, and the cocoa business had not shown signs of slowing down.

Prominent rulers in the western area of the lower Guinea Region, including King Adéorí, had begun high-level coordination and a coalition to build their strength ahead of negotiations with European trading companies. King Adéorí had also created and enacted a European trading advisory council, which consisted of a few members of his council and other prominent businessmen in his kingdom. This council was the first of its kind, and rulers from neighbouring kingdoms followed suit with the same strategy. Adéorí was known to think far ahead, and everyone knew he intended to prosper from all deals made for the benefit of his people. A few foreign companies had begun to visit, and the King and his council had been busy receiving them from far and near.

Adénìké's disposition and attitude had also begun to brighten. She was slowly returning to her normal self, coming out of her chambers frequently, on good terms with the King, and fully engaging with the women's empowerment activities she had created. It had taken some time for her to understand that the King had not in any way planned to make her unhappy. If she had listened to him, none of the unfortunate events would have happened, and she took responsibility for her actions. She had also made a conscious effort to build a good relationship with the new queen by involving her in the women's empowerment program. The King was happy about that, and he had commended her for her openness, understanding, and maturity.

Queen Adénìké had also tried to stop seeing Oláolú since their last encounter in Ede, but the task had been a difficult one for her to handle. She craved his presence and found it hard to control her emotions and the urge to feel his body close to hers. Sometimes, she wondered whether what she felt for him was love or an intense physical attraction powered by lust. At times, she'd almost convinced herself to orchestrate a day trip out of the kingdom so she and Oláolú could spend some time together. Other times, she felt tempted to ask her maidens to fetch him so she could at least touch him and get ahold of him in her chambers. Each time, she would weigh her options and decide she did not want to take the risk of the King ever finding out that she had been unfaithful.

She alone knew that her urge to be with Oláolú had constituted more than half of the reason she had disobeyed the King and visited Ede, which had led to the King's marriage to another wife. These thoughts continued to linger in her mind, and her deepest fear was that she might cause her own downfall as a queen in the kingdom by continuing to see Oláolú and harbour these feelings for him.

One morning in late November, Queen Adénìké felt nauseous and ill. A few of the palace staff and one of her private maidens were reportedly sick with the mild flu that was spreading throughout the kingdom. It did not appear serious enough to worry about as people often contracted some form of it during that time of year, when the harmattan winds begin to blow. No one aside from the two maidens who had worked directly in her chambers knew how she felt. Adénìké was very healthy, and she never fell ill, so her maidens were surprised to see how pale and tired she looked that evening.

They prepared chicken soup for her, along with some fruit to help her feel better. Barely five minutes after she'd eaten half of the soup, she felt uncomfortable and had to run to the washbasin to vomit everything she'd taken in. The maidens became worried, and she was beginning to worry, as well. She rarely fell ill, even when others did, and vomiting was completely unheard of for her.

The maidens expressed their concern to the Queen. 'I am so sorry, My Queen. How do you feel, Your Majesty?' asked the first maiden.

The second maiden left to get a warm bowl of water. She returned and handed the bowl to Adénìké who washed her face a few times, gargled the warm water in her mouth, and spat it out. 'Thank you, dear,' said the Queen as she handed the bowl back to the maiden. 'I think I feel better now.'

'You are welcome, My Queen,' the maiden replied. 'Do you want me to inform the King about your health, Your Majesty?'

Queen Adénìké snapped back, 'Why do you want to inform the King? Is the King a doctor or a medicine man?'

'I am sorry, My Queen.'

'Go and fetch me the *Ìyá alágbo* (the mother of herbal concussion medicine),' ordered Queen Adénìké. 'Tell her to please return with you immediately, or as soon as she is able.'

'Certainly, My Queen,' responded the maiden. She left immediately to fetch Ìyá *alágbo*.

Queen Adénìké walked back to her private chambers. She sat for a moment, took a bite of an orange slice that had been brought in, and lay down to rest quietly. She felt uncomfortable and wondered how she might have caught the flu. Her knees and arms felt weak, but she kept telling herself that everything would be fine.

Forty-five minutes later, a knock on Adénìké's private chambers' door woke her up. She had napped for some time. Her maiden said that Ìyá alágbo was there to see her, and Queen Adénìké who was still feeling tired, sat up in her bed and asked them to come in.

The maiden held open the door for an elegantly dressed, elderly woman with grey hair. Ìyá alágbo uttered some prayers and incantations before entering the room, followed by the maiden. Ìyá alágbo was popular in the kingdom for prescribing the best herbal medicines and concoctions, and she had been summoned to the palace a few times in the past. She was passionate about the royal family because of the stories she had heard from her parents and grandparents about how very kind the royal family had been to their family in the past. That citizens of Ìkirè Kingdom loved the royal family was not news; King Adéorí was considered a true son of the land and the love of his people.

'*Àláàfià fún oní ilé* (peace be upon the owner of this home),' said Ìyá alágbo.

'*Ekú àrò, ma* (good morning, ma),' Queen Adénìké replied.

'*Ekú àrò aya oba* (good morning, wife of the King). How are you, My Queen?'

'I am not well, mama. I've felt terrible all morning.' The Queen waved at the maiden to excuse herself. After the maiden had departed, she said to Ìyá alágbo, 'I feel very weak, and I cannot eat anything.'

'*Olórun yíò fún o ní àláfíà láìpé* (The Almighty will grant you good health very soon),' the older woman replied soothingly. 'Please, lay down on your back, My Queen, while I examine you.'

Queen Adénìké lay down, and Ìyá alágbo examined her eyes, then her mouth, her abdomen, and her feet. After several minutes of examination, Ìyá alágbo covered the Queen with a blanket and sat down on the stool beside the bed.

'My Queen, I have a question,' Ìyá alágbo stated carefully. 'When last did you experience your monthly menstrual cycle?'

Queen Adénìké's face froze in shock. It was the last thing she'd expected to hear from Ìyá alágbo, and her heart raced furiously. 'My mind has been occupied with many concerns lately, mama. I think it was about eight weeks or so ago, if I am not mistaken. Am I pregnant, mama?' she asked fearfully, worry building up inside her.

'Yes, My Queen,' answered the older woman. 'I can't be absolutely certain yet, but I do believe you are pregnant. This is great news for our kingdom, My Queen.'

Queen Adénìké broke into tears when Ìyá alágbo confirmed the most terrifying news of which she could have ever dreamt. The healer assumed they were tears of joy. She had no suspicion they were really tears of agony, pain, and sorrow.

The Queen could no longer hold herself back. She knew that she had not slept with the King in many months, and the only man with whom she had been was Oláolú.

She realised that she needed to restrain herself in front of the healer. 'Thank you, mama. Please, keep my pregnancy a secret for now, and do not tell anyone.'

Ìyá alágbo replied respectfully, '*Béèni aya oba, eni tó ni oyún ló ni ohùn* (yes, wife of the King, the person who owns the pregnancy owns the voice). You have my word. It will remain a secret until you and the palace are ready to reveal the news to the kingdom. As soon as I get home, I will send my daughter, Atinúké, to bring you some herbs this evening. Take them every morning when you wake up and at night before you sleep. Please, do not hesitate to send for me if you need anything, My Queen. I will take my leave now.' The older woman got up from the stool and withdrew from the Queen's private chambers.

Still in disbelief about what she had just heard, Queen Adéníké fell down on her knees and wept bitterly. What could be worse than this? she wondered. Her grief and tears flowed freely, and she couldn't stop wondering how she had allowed herself to end up in this abominable situation.

Asèsè ń mú eye bò lápò - The story has just begun.

GLOSSARY

Ìkirè Kingdom, lower Guinea Region, Africa: southern region of modern-day Nigeria.

Yoruba – English

asèsè ń mú eye bò lápò – the story has just begun

adúpé – thank you

agbenu òrìsà ńlá – mouthpiece of the gods

àgbo – herbal tea

ajá tó ma sonù kò ní gbó fèrè olóde – the dog that goes missing will never hear the whistle of the hunter

àlááfià fún oní ilé – peace be upon the owner of this home

alágbára – the powerful

alágbára láriń erú – most powerful amongst slaves

amóba rérìń – one who makes the King smile

àse – amen; so shall it be

113

aya oba – wife of the King

babaláwo – father of the mysteries

balógun – the chief warrior and generalissimo

báwo ni aya oba? – how are you, My Queen?

báwo ni òré mi – how are you, my friend

bééni aya oba, eni tó ni oyún ló ni ohùn – yes, wife of the King, the person who owns the pregnancy owns the voice

dòdò ìkirè – plantain bites

ègúsí – melon soup

ekálé baba mi – good evening, my father

ekú árò aya oba – good morning, wife of the King

ekú árò, ma – good morning, ma

ekú ilé olówó orí mi – greetings to the owner and payer of my bride price

elènu màrí màso – the one whose mouth says everything that is seen

èmi ò lówó ní nuè – I do not support it

eni tóbá bèrè ònà kò ní shi ònàgbà – the person who asks for directions will not go in the wrong direction

eni tóbá wo bàtà lómo ibi tí bàtà tiń ta lésè – it is the person who wears the shoes that knows where they hurt the feet

esé – thank you

èwò – abomination

ibi líle latí ń bá okùnrin – in the tough places are where we find a man

ìgboràn sán ju ebo rúrú lo – no type of ritual performed to solve a problem is better than being obedient and avoiding the problem in the first place.

igi gogoro má gùn mi lójú, àti òkèrè latí ń wó bò – we don't want a sharp stick in our eyes, but the only way this could eventually happen is if we kept looking at it

ìrùkèrè – fly whisks made of horsehair strands fastened to a stick by a leather handle

ìyá alágbo – the mother of herbal concussion medicine

iya mi – my mother

iyán – pounded yam

ìyàwó – junior wife

kabiyesi o – one who does not yield or surrender to anyone

kókó – lumps

kònkòn – traditional sponge

kú àbò aya oba – welcome back, wife of the King

mama mi – my mother

mo ní ìfé re gidi gan – I love you very much

mo sùn dada – I slept very well

ní agbára olódùmarè, èsè baaba kò ní gbérí kó tún wá se
lórí omo o – by the power of The Almighty, the
sins of the father shall not surface and then manifest on the sons

nkan tí àgbàlagbà ńrí tí o bá jòkó sí abé igi òpe, omodé ò
le ri tí óbá gun orí igi òpe kań nà – what an elder
sees from merely sitting at the bottom of a palm
tree, a child cannot see even if they climb to the
top of the palm tree

nkan tó bá ti yá kì tún pé mó – once it is time to do something, there is no reason for any more delays

oba – king; Your Majesty

oba wa olúbùsólá àti gbogbo àwon ìgbìmò ìlú mo kí yiń
ó – Our King, the one ordained by God to wealth,
and all the council member chiefs: I greet you all

òdèré kókò – palm doves

ojú lòró wà – when the eyes meet is when real conversation happens

oko wa – our husband

okùnrin méta – three men in one

olódùmarè – The Almighty

olorì àgbà – older queen

olórí àwon ìgbìmò ìlú – head of the council of chiefs

olorì aya oba – Queen and wife of the King

olórun yíò fún o ní àláfíà láìpé – The Almighty will grant
you good health very soon

olówó orí mi – the one who paid and owns my dowry

omo tí wón kó dada tí ó tún ara rè kó – a child that was
properly raised who heeded advice and also
thought well of herself

ose dúdú – black soap

òtún oba – the right hand of the King

ó ye kí o mò wípé sùúrù lérè – you should know that
patience is a virtue

wákàtì meta – three hours

ABOUT THE AUTHOR

Born in Lagos Nigeria, Babatunde Olaniran established the foundation of his legacy at a very young age. He learned loyalty as he grew up amongst his cousins. He established integrity that he earned from his relatives and grew unconditional love for humanity with the many personal encounters he had while living in Nigeria. All of this has given Babatunde a passion towards humanity and a purpose to serve all people.

Babatunde did not only have a strong foundation at home. He attended the prestigious King's College Lagos where he earned is Senior Secondary School Certificate before proceeding to earning a diploma in electrical electronic engineering, a bachelor's degree in Project Management Technology and an MBA with project management specialization. He is also a certified PMP (Project Management Professional)

Also Babatunde explored food production as an additional trade while in school and merged his technology, management and engineering training experience to help expand his family's agricultural food processing business into the export market in the west. He co-founded a software technology company with a few friends from business school and he is also an active partner at BiiLGroup. A Nigerian Investment Company.

Babatunde enjoys writing, playing football, taking walks/runs and spending quality time with friends and family. To learn more, you can visit www.olaniran.com

Báa pé láyé, àá dìtàn, bá ò pé láyé àá dìtàn

(If we live long, we'll become history; if we don't live long, we'll still become history)

 www.babatundeolaniran.com

 babatundeolaniran_

 TundeSpeaks

9 781913 674496